# HOW TO WIN THE WORLD SERIES
## OF POKER (OR NOT)

PAT WALSH was previously a senior editor of the independent publisher MacAdam/Cage, and before that a reporter for the *San Francisco Chronicle*. The author of *78 Reasons Why Your Book May Never Be Published and 14 Reasons Why It Just Might* (Penguin), he lives in San Francisco.

AN ALL-AMERICAN TALE

# How to Win the World Series of Poker

## of Poker

(or Not)

# PAT WALSH

ROBSON
BOOKS

First published in Great Britain in 2006 by
Robson Books
151 Freston Road
London
W10 6TH

An imprint of Anova Books Company Ltd

Published in the United States by Plume, a member of Penguin Group (USA) in 2006

ISBN 1 86105 962 0

10 9 8 7 6 5 4 3 2 1

Printed and bound by MPG Books Ltd, Bodmin, Cornwall

This book can be ordered direct from the publisher
Contact the marketing department, but try your bookshop first

www.anovabooks.com

*For Jeannine, my very own royal flush*

"The next best thing to gambling and winning is gambling and losing."

—Nick "the Greek" Dandalos

# Contents

# How to Win the World Series of Poker
## (or Not)

# Texas Hold 'em How-To

**It is said** of Texas Hold 'em that it takes a minute to learn and a lifetime to master. This is not true. It takes about ten minutes to learn and it cannot be mastered, ever.

A reasonable person might assume that anyone reading a book titled *How to Win the World Series of Poker* would already know the basics of Texas Hold 'em. I am not, in this regard and many others, a reasonable person. The first book I ever read on the subject was *Tournament Poker for Advanced Players*. Below is a brief primer on the game of No-Limit Texas Hold 'em.

Limit Hold 'em restricts the size of players' bets. In a $4/$8 game, the limit is $4 for the first two rounds and then double that for the final two. During the early rounds, if a player wants to bet, he can only bet $4. If someone wants to raise, he can only raise $4. Betting in no-limit is restricted only by the amount of chips you have in front of you, and the minimum bet is the amount previously bet by another player or the size of the big blind. The ability to bet everything you have, going all-in, at any time, is what makes the game, and the people who play it, dangerous and sexy.

Hold 'em is a variation on Seven-Card Stud, meaning there is no drawing additional cards from the deck, and each player has seven cards from which to make the best five-card hand.

The variant that makes Hold 'em special is that instead of having seven of his own cards to work with, each player gets only two cards for his exclusive use. The other five cards are shared by all the players. Sharing may be nice in kindergarten, but it can be awful in poker.

Like all poker games, the position of dealer is passed in a clockwise direction. In private games, the deck is simply passed from one player to another. In a casino or card room, a professional dealer tosses all the cards, but a plastic puck, called the button, rotates around the table, designating who would be the dealer if players were trusted to touch the deck.

Most card games have an ante, but Hold 'em uses blinds instead. The person to the dealer's left has to put forth a bet called the small blind, and the person to his left is forced to put up a bigger bet, called the big blind. The bets are called blinds because they have to be made before the players see any cards.

Every player gets two cards, and only two cards, dealt to them. Since the blinds have already bet, the next player to the left is the next to act. He has, like all players still in the hand, three options. He can call the big blind bet, raise any amount equal to or greater than the big blind, or fold. After he has acted, the turn, or action, moves to the next player. If no one calls, the big blind takes the pot. If there is a raise at any point, the action continues around the table until everyone has either folded or put the same amount of money in the pot. If there are only calls and no raises, then the big blind can still raise if he sees fit. This is called a live blind.

When the pot is right, the dealer will burn the top card—that is, remove it from play by putting it to the side, where folded and out-of-play hands are gathered, called the muck.

The dealer will then expose three cards faceup. This is called the flop. Since five cards are now available for each player to view (the three cards from the flop and each player's two hole cards), most players know what hands they are hoping for and will try to ascertain how the flop helped their opponents. There is another round of betting, beginning now with the small blind seat and ending with the dealer. Then another single card, called the turn, or fourth street, will be exposed, followed by another round of betting. The river, or final card, is then flipped up, and more betting ensues.

During all rounds, each player is trying to establish if his hand is, or likely will be, the strongest when all is said and done.

When all the betting action has subsided and more than one player is still active, hands are turned over, and the person with the highest hand takes the money. If, as sometimes happens, there is a tie, the active players split the pot. Then you start over and do it again. Whee!

**In a poker tournament,** each player starts with the same amount of chips. The blinds start relatively small but rise every period, generally every half hour or hour. This prevents people from sitting and waiting for the best hands and forces them to play more hands. Some players will increase their chips, while others will lose everything. Players who lose all their chips leave the tournament, and tables are combined. Eventually, a predetermined number of players will survive long enough to be included in the prize pool. This is generally 10 percent of the entrants. When all but nine or ten are gone, a final table is put together. The percentage of prize money a player receives increases the longer he survives.

In the 2005 World Series of Poker, there were 5,619 entrants, and 560 players made it into the money. This means 5,059 people paid $10,000 each to enter and left with nothing but a bad-beat story. But the winner received $7,500,000.

# Prologue

**The lamb that thinks** he's a lion is the mother's milk of gamblers, and I intend to prove this tonight. I'm sitting at the table and doing very well. I have more chips at the table than anyone else, save one. A player who calls himself Mr. Fish has a slight lead over me, but not for long. I started this game of Texas Hold 'em with a small stack of chips and built a huge pile by playing smart, aggressive poker. The few times I went all-in, I did so in a way that implied weakness, inviting callers. When I bluffed, I did it perfectly, so that everyone folded before I had to show my cards. I am playing what I believe to be perfect poker.

I ask Mr. Fish if his name is an homage to Abe Vigoda, but he ignores me completely. I am amused and honored that he feels even answering my question will give me ammunition against him on the felt. We haven't tangled together much tonight, but I know it's just a matter of time. I've been running all over this table and he's stayed out of my way, only getting involved with pots that I've passed over. The two times we were in together, he folded when I raised. I know he's sitting there waiting until he gets a great hand, and then he'll try to suck me in.

The moment finally comes when another player known as the Tuxedo bets before me and I'm holding two aces, the best possible opening hand. Mr. Fish has yet to bet, and I make a little raise of fifty chips, like I'm trying to steal the pot, which I've done many times tonight. Mr. Fish takes the bait and makes a big raise of two hundred chips, causing the Tuxedo to fold like a cheap suit (sorry). I'm afraid that if I raise again, Mr. Fish will drop out too, and I want more of his money. I just call.

The flop is a queen of spades, a queen of hearts, and an ace of spades, giving me a full house, one of the best possible hands. I don't want to scare Mr. Fish off, so I check. He makes a large bet of four hundred chips, and I wait for a moment and then raise him another four hundred. He thinks for a moment and calls. I figure that his hand is either two high spades, like the king and queen, giving him three of a kind and a high flush draw, or an ace/queen, giving him a full house, but a lower one than mine. The next card comes, and it's a three of clubs, which couldn't have helped him. I want him to make his flush so I can get him to bet or call, so I check again. He checks too. The river card is a ten of spades, and I'm as happy as Donny Most being recognized in an airport bar.

I figure he's made his hand now and has so many chips in the pot that he's not going to back down. So I bet everything I have and smile like a smart-ass. Mr. Fish immediately calls. Something is not right. His hole cards turn over and flash a pair of queens, giving him four of a kind and me a terrible case of heartburn. A little computerized voice buzzes, *Bad beat.*

I'm stunned and drunk with rage. There is only one option left to me. I punch my computer screen, leaving a permanent mark to taunt me until I can afford to buy a new laptop, which by the looks of things won't be anytime soon. A minute ago I ruled the poker savanna. I tried to let out a roar, but the only thing that came out was a resounding bleat.

When you lose all your money, you immediately curse yourself for not quitting while you were ahead. This logic is valuable only in retrospect because, when you're winning, there is no fixed point of how much more you can win. Losing, however, has a final resting point: zero. I am at zero.

Waxing philosophic on poker is as tempting to the writer as it is boring to the reader. Suffice it to say, the enigma of poker is not that it is hard; the problem is that it is incredibly easy, which entices the greedy and those who feed off the greedy. Keeping with this dichotomy, Texas Hold 'em is the easiest game to learn, therefore the most beguiling to play. Various poker playing styles are successful if they are consistent. The professionals have a simple law: The more you remove luck, the more money you will make. Pros disdain the person who wins at the slots because winning money is a serious thing, not to be left to chance. It must be earned. The game of No-Limit Texas Hold 'em is the premier poker variant, favored by the best, smartest, bravest, and shrewdest players because at any point you can lose all your chips or take all of someone else's. For the same reasons, the game attracts the greediest, most reckless, and dumbest players to the tables. This is where I come in.

I lean back from the table, the real table, my kitchen table. I let my hands draw back from the keyboard, which is at once relieving and unnatural since they've been stretched in front of me for so long. The computer screen says I have no money left in my account, and after fifteen seconds, the game goes on without me. The only evidence I was ever in the game is Mr. Fish's fat chip count. I muster some pride and gamesmanship and type the words *Nice hand. Good luck all* on the chat board. Mr. Fish finally breaks his silence to respond with *GG*, which I've learned means *good game*. But what he's really saying is, *So long, sucker!*

Casinos may not have clocks, but I have one right in front of me. It's made of papier-mâché and red paint. My four-year-old son made it for me in his preschool class, and it says it is two thirty in the morning.

I release a noise from my throat that is part sigh and part plea for the sweet release that death might bring. My rattle must have been louder than I thought because momentarily my wife walks into the kitchen. She asks sweetly if I won or lost, and I must fight the instinct to get unreasonably upset. I know it's wrong to get mad at a loved one for something you did wrong, but it feels so right, at least for a moment. One of the great things about being a married man is being able to survive the occasional act of idiocy. Dating, at least for me, was hell because I had to go long periods without doing anything really stupid.

*Come to bed,* she says warmly. I shut off the computer and follow her. She's walking ahead of me to the bedroom, turning out all the lights, and I know now that she's not going to ask if I won or lost again because she already knows. For her, the details can wait till morning, but not for me.

*I lost everything,* I say.

She turns around, and even in the absence of light I see panic like an infrared glow from her face.

*I mean everything in my new online account. Six dollars and forty cents. I was playing in the penny-ante games and I was way up, and then this guy called Mr. Fish . . .*

*You spent all night playing poker for pennies!?*

Is she really mad at me because I didn't lose enough? If losing big is all it takes to make her happy, boy, did I marry the right woman.

*Hey, it's my job.*

Writing about poker involves thinking about poker, reading about poker, and especially playing poker. This thought might seem intuitive, but it is a truism my wife cannot see. Her mind follows a different line of logical thinking: Poker is a game and games are recreation; writing is a job and jobs are work. Therefore, playing poker is not writing, and it certainly isn't working. When I stay up late playing online, or run off to a game, there's always a skeptical tinge in her voice when she says good night or good-bye.

I know this in the way long-married people know what their

spouse is thinking from the tiny inflections and subtle gestures that have become ingrained in our heads. Over dinner, my wife could turn to me and say, *Where did we put that thing?*

*What thing?* I'll say.

*You know, that thing.*

*Do you mean the candelabra made from driftwood that my mom gave us for Christmas six years ago?*

*Yeah, that thing.*

At no time is this type of interaction more evident than when other people are present, making it impossible, or at least socially awkward, to be blunt.

*Honey, I'm a little tired, are you ready to go home?* really means *Put that beer down and get in the taxi.* Just as *I hate this twisty road* means *You are driving like a fucking madman.*

So when my wife wakes to an empty bed and finds me in the kitchen playing online, she will simply say, *Are you still playing poker?* I'll hear her true message: *Shouldn't you be in bed with your wife rather than gambling the mortgage payment away to a guy named pokergod69?*

I'll mumble, *I'll be in bed in two seconds.* Meaning, of course, *See you at dawn.*

If you are not married or, at least, in a long-term hippielike life commitment, then you cannot understand this phenomenon. When you live with someone for a long time, she gets into your head, where, at times, two is a crowd.

I've only seen my own parents fight three times, and all three instances were over a game of Scrabble. My dad would try to use a Gaelic word, and my mother, overly fond of the English language, would balk. Likewise, my mother was not above making up words, such as adding the letter *s* to *paint* to make *spaint*. When queried, she'd have a perfectly sound definition at the ready. *You don't know spaint?*—quickly grabbing more tiles—*A spaint is a miniature tool, used in making dollhouse furniture.*

I can only imagine what would happen if a husband and wife

wound up head-to-head at a high-stakes final table. The game would last a very long time, and at the end of it a very rich person would be sleeping on the couch.

All the big poker pros are married, and, from what I've watched and read, have surprisingly traditional home lives with ranch houses, kids in school, and payments to make. That they work in card rooms and casinos is merely incidental. They view their profession as a job, and they quantify their success by how much they make an hour playing cards, after expenses.

Though most gamblers aren't disciplined, professional poker players are paragons of restraint. They exude self-control and patience. The reason their home lives have such stability is that they can budget their time like it is money, they can manage impulses. They can also read their spouses' moods and respond accordingly.

Standing in the doorway to our bedroom, I decide not to tell my wife about the many attributes held by professional poker players because she will point out, correctly, that I have few of these qualities. I have a gambler's discipline, not a poker player's. I think about how many ways I can win, not how I might lose. Las Vegas was built by and for guys like me, and I'd live there except I can't stand the heat or the fashion.

*Hey, it takes a long time to lose ten dollars playing for pennies,* I say.

This does not soothe her. *Come to bed,* she says again, but this time there is no sympathy. I crawl into bed with one thought in my head: Mr. Fish must be destroyed. It then occurs to me briefly that losing was my fault and I should learn from it, or at least brush it off. But I'm too tired to be mad at myself, so instead I start dreaming of beating Mr. Fish to a pulp and taking his last dime and leaving him to be eaten by wild chickens, if such things exist. This thought warms me, and I vow to myself that I will eventually get this guy, right after I fulfill my new vocational mission—winning the World Series of Poker. Right now, though, winning millions of dollars and achieving poker glory seem paltry compared to beating Mr. Fish.

My first day as a professional poker player is over, and I'm going to bed—and I'm going to bed a loser.

 **Poker,** and specifically Texas Hold 'em, is the quintessential American game, a national institution like mom, apple pie, and dipping things in ranch dressing. In Hold 'em, you don't have to have the best cards to win as long as you have the biggest stones, and you don't have to always be the smartest player as long as you're the luckiest when you need to be. What other game pits hubris against math on a level field? A good poker player is an amalgamation of smart, ballsy, shrewd, cunning, and lucky, and is, most important, a natural winner. Not coincidentally, this is how almost all Americans think of themselves. The best part of Hold 'em is that not only can you lie, it's practically required. We, as a people, love to lie, especially for money and fame. I am no exception.

It was with this in mind that I decided to announce my intention to win the World Series of Poker.

The World Series of Poker is a single-elimination, freeze-out tournament with a $10,000 buy-in that takes place each summer in Las Vegas. This means that every entrant pays $10,000 for a stack of poker chips and plays cards until all his chips are gone. Eventually, there is one player with everyone else's money.

Once you're broke, protocol dictates you grab your coat, shake the hand of the player who took the last of your dough, and walk out, preferably without looking back. The best players leave the room like they have something better or more important to do. All this, of course, is to mask that they have just donated ten grand to someone else and had their dreams crushed by a single mistake, a bad decision, or just plain shitty luck.

The upside is that the winner takes home a garish bracelet. Oh, and many millions of dollars. But he or she isn't the only one who takes home cash. The more players that go broke before you, the more you move up the ladder, and if you last long enough, you get a piece of the prize pool. It's called being in the money. The higher you place in the tournament, the bigger your share.

The moment a poker player decides he is ready to enter the World Series of Poker is a turning point in his life. His mathematical skills, impulse control, and self-confidence must be at peak levels. It takes years of observing the body language of other players and reading tells—the little twitches, tics, and expressions—that betray their cards' strengths or weaknesses. Meanwhile, he must train himself to betray nothing of his own hands.

He must be certain that he is a contender before paying the $10,000 entry fee. He must be at the top of his game and feel he has a shot to win it. Or he can wing it and say, *What the fuck.* There are no guarantees except one: You cannot win if you don't play. Gambling has thrived on the governing principles that reward is proportional to risk and that those people who take the biggest risks are either champs or chumps. There's something to be said for both philosophies, but I've always been partial to the latter although I aspire to the former.

**There is only one picture** of me in my 1985 high school yearbook. I'm seated at a table playing Texas Hold 'em in a mock World Series of Poker. I'm wearing a suit jacket, a religious collar, and a fedora because I'm supposed to be playing the part of a Southern preacher. The others at the table are also in costume—a cowboy, a biker, a slick Johnny Vegas type—but none are quite as absurd as me in my getup. Why we were playing poker in English class, especially a game that was as relatively unknown at the time as Hold 'em, is now lost to me. It probably had something to do with making characters in literature come to life, or creating a scene for the basis of an essay, or a living metaphor for the boredom of high school English teachers.

What I do remember, or what I think I remember, is that I won the tournament. I can't say for certain, given the number of years that have passed, but I'm pretty sure I won. Certainly, in the yearbook picture, I'm the only one smiling.

It'd be nice to remember if I won my first tournament, but it doesn't matter. It's great enough to be able to say, when asked, that I've been playing competitive Hold 'em for almost twenty years. I do not mention that there were nineteen years between my first game of Hold 'em and my second. Just having been aware of the game back when A Flock of Seagulls had a promising career in front of them makes me feel that I have an advantage over others, but it's a benefit I've abused for too long.

My wife endures my love of poker. She knows I hog all the TiVo hours with tournaments. She thoughtfully listens to me bitch and moan about never having a game at our house before reminding me that the reason we don't host many games is because I keep canceling them due to work travel or because I forget to call and invite people until it's too late.

She likes poker too, but her idea of a game is slightly different from mine. She buys fresh flowers and spends the daylight hours cleaning the house—simply because people are coming over. *There're not people, they're poker players. They don't care if the house is knee-deep in sewage as long as the game is fair. It's a poker game, not a dinner party,* I tell her. *People should smoke, swear, and, perhaps, belch.* She just smiles and sends me out to buy slabs of

Brie and Camembert for the cheese plate. Let me say that cheese—good cheese—isn't cheap. I start every home game in the hole sixty bucks just because we have to have something made from a liquid by-product of a goat on a platter. The cheese costs so much that I believe milking goats must be one of the best-paying jobs out there.

When we do have a game, it's damn slow to start. There's always an hour and a half of chitchat and *Can I get your coat?* and *What would you like to drink?* and *Congratulations on having triplets* and all this other bullshit before we can sit down and play. Then I explain the rules of Texas Hold 'em, and someone always says, *What's wild?* or *Can't we play dealer's choice?* I respond with my spiel about how Hold 'em is the perfect game because it favors the really smart and the really lucky, and everyone considers themselves a member of one of those two groups. So we start to deal.

My moment of clarity came to me after hosting just such a game with several friends and some people who pretend to be my friends because they like my wife. I counted out the chips, and we all sat down to play Texas Hold 'em. I had half the chips at the table before I had to show anyone my cards. Beating your own game is easier than you might think, because controlling the guest list lets you have more information than any other player. You know who's afraid to lose their buy-in and will play tight, and who just wants a night of drinking beer and doesn't care about the money. You know who is a liar at heart and who is true to a fault. If I've never played with a particular guest, I can still figure it out. If they are my friends, they're probably liars, and if they're my wife's kith and kin, then they are most likely on the square.

By the end of the night, I had more than 80 percent of the money brought to the table, and I felt like my dingus was three feet long. Regardless of having an edge beforehand, I was thrilled to take down the game by using smart play and aggressive betting. I didn't even care when one very dear friend complained about my constant raises, saying I was taking the fun out of the game. *What are you talking about*, I protested, *this is a veritable funfest. The only bad thing is that my arms are getting tired from raking in all the chips.* I'm going to miss knowing him.

The turning point in my relationship with poker came when I was dealt the three and five of clubs. It's not a good hand by anyone's measure, but I was on a roll and wanted to play, so I called the $4 blind. Several other players called and the flop was dealt: ace of clubs, two of clubs, four of clubs. I had flopped a straight flush, the best possible hand. The odds of this happening, if my math is correct, are a gazillion point six to one. Because I'd been bluffing a lot, I couldn't just check without making everyone suspicious. So I made a sizable bet and hoped I was called a liar. Several others folded before the action came to rest on a friend's wife, who had never played poker before this night. She had lost every single hand and made several horrible mistakes, like folding instead of checking and betting out of turn. She was, however, a delight who congratulated every player who won a pot and refilled everyone's cocktail every time she got up. She peeked at her cards and did everything but yell *Yahoo!* She asked if she could show her cards to her husband for advice. I said sure. He looked at her cards and then the flop and whispered in her ear. She smiled and pushed in all her chips. My one-in-a-million hand now presented a moral dilemma. I could call her bet, make a fool of her, ruin her night, and put her last $20 in my pocket. Or I could be a mensch and fold my hand, letting her be the one at the table who took down the big bully. She would undoubtedly receive a round of applause and beam with pride. Only I would have to know of my altruism, and I'd sleep like a baby that night.

I called her bet and took her money.

I didn't do it for the money, and I didn't do it just to be an asshole, although that's what everyone else thought. I did it because I wanted to take the game seriously, regardless of consequences, and to do that, I couldn't pull any punches. When I thought about the whole thing later, I realized that if I was going to be a coldhearted son of a bitch, I should do it where it would be understood, even respected. I resolved to start playing poker at a level where there is no guilt in winning at any cost.

In a way, I consider it my first real poker game. I had played scores of games before, but I had always lost. I always had an excuse, such as drinking during the game, often to excess, or discounting smart play because the stakes were too low or making bad calls because I was annoyed with—or hated with a passion— the other bettor. I told myself, *Losing doesn't matter because you know what you did wrong. You only made those mistakes because winning didn't actually matter. Having fun and boozing it up or upstaging a guy you think is a dick was more important.* But I was sick of losing.

I may not be a great poker player, but I share the only truly essential element all professional poker players have in common: I love other people's money. I love other people's money more than the other people love it, and I want their money more than they want mine. This, I believe, is the seed from which grows the mighty high-stakes gambler. I believe, if given the chance, I can be a championship poker player, and I decided that I must try.

I am not, however, the sole master of my fate. There is another critical point in the life of a poker player who has decided to enter the World Series of Poker: telling his wife.

My wife is supportive of my endeavors, even the strange ones. For my birthday she gave me a gift certificate for fencing lessons after I mentioned wanting to take one last stab at winning an Olympic gold medal. I ended up never taking the lessons because I learned bowling was a medal sport, buying me ten or twenty years to hit the lanes and go for the gold. She is also generous to a fault, as evidenced one Christmas when she gave me a very expensive new belt, even though I lose belts with alarming regularity at airport security checkpoints. I mean, it was like flushing money down the toilet.

Asking her to let me spend many thousands of dollars on what, optimistically, could be called a pipe dream was going to stretch the limits of even her kindness.

My concerns seemed insurmountable. Reason and prudence were going to win this battle, and this bothered me to no end. Rational thoughts, however, cannot breach self-pity, at least with most men. So I did what husbands do when something is eating us up inside: I sank into a bitter mood of feeling sorry for myself. After a few days of my stomping and sulking around the house and snapping at her for the oddest of reasons, my wife demanded to know what specific genus of bug had crawled up my butt.

*What the hell,* I thought.

I told her we needed to talk about something that was important to me.

*We're not getting a dog,* she said.

*Not that. I have a . . . what's the word . . . fantasy I want to talk to you about.*

*Sweetie, we talked about this before we were married.*

*Not that either. Unless you've become more open-minded?*

*Ain't going to happen.*

*Fine. But I'm talking about something else. I want to play in the World Series of Poker.*

My wife is used to my little obsessions, and after ten years of marriage she's well-schooled in dealing with them. We all have a jones at any given time. Mine was poker, at least right now. It could be monster trucks or herbal high colonics tomorrow, but right now it was poker, specifically No-Limit Texas Hold 'em. It didn't surprise me, then, that her reaction was composed. I began outlining my plan, addressing concerns while still emphasizing the positives. I made my arguments, and they were good arguments. They had style, aplomb, and, if I do say so, gravitas. I talked of making dreams come true, shooting the moon, making millions, and becoming a more fulfilled man and therefore a better husband. I began gushing about my love of poker, my increasing skill, all the books I'd read, my excellent strategy. My earnest spewing forth must have had an effect because she listened patiently and even gave me a couple of sympathetic nods. When I was finished, she smiled and said nine glorious words.

*If it's important to you, you should do it.*

I kissed her so quickly she barely got the last word out. I was so flushed with gratitude that I got up and instantly decided to clean the bathrooms, something she claims I never do. I was about to inquire about where the household cleaning supplies were kept when she added nine more words.

*Do you have a plan to pay for it?*

*It's only ten grand,* I said.

*It's only ten grand,* she repeated, but in a very different tone of voice. It really sounded better when I said it.

She was, of course, right. Ten thousand dollars is a lot of money. We have a child, a mortgage, car payments, video store late fees, and many other financial commitments. My old foe, reality, had once again arrived.

Desperate, I started musing on all the ways we might get the money. *How much room is on the credit cards for cash advances? How much is in our son's college fund? Having a car in the city is really a pain in the ass, don't you think? Do we really need this big house? Is an engagement ring still essential after the marriage? Hypothetically, if one wanted to sell a kidney, where would one go, do you think?*

My wife suggested writing a book about poker and using the advance as a stake. I took this simple but brilliant suggestion in and let it swirl around my greedy brain. I had already written a book containing everything I knew about my job in publishing, so unless someone wanted to buy a book about the other things I'm good at—namely, programming my TiVo and making pancakes with meat in them—there was no sequel possibility. It occurred to me that if I was going to use the book money for cards, I should write a book about poker. I originally thought *How to Win the World Series of Poker* could be an analytic and scientific delineation of an unbeatable strategy for winning poker's highest honor, but I soon realized that would take a lot of experience, which I don't have, and a lot of hard work, which I'm averse to.

I mulled briefly over writing a history of poker, but every book about poker has a chapter or section on the origin of the game and how it got its name, et cetera. Who cares? Suffice it to say, the game began somewhere else and was called something else, eventually becoming perverted or perfected, depending on your point of view, into the game it is today.

I considered anthologies, compilations, and collections until I realized they were all the same thing, and a nightmare of legal paperwork besides. I started running all these concepts past my wife, who was less than impressed. As a last resort, I turned to simplicity and pitched my idea.

*What if I write a good old American story about an average schmo making a stab at the World Series of Poker? After all, it's the only championship that anyone can compete for without qualifying. It could be an underdog story, like* Rocky, *without the push-ups or the physical pain. A chronicle of my poker journey from working stiff and beleaguered family man by day . . .*

*Beleaguered?*

*I meant beloved. A beloved family man who plays in every game he can find on the road to winning the World Series of Poker. What do you think? I asked.*

*Good luck.*

**My journey** to the final table of the World Series of Poker was only a few days old and already I had learned three unexpected but important poker lessons.

The first lesson was that I am an idiot.

The second was that "Mike" can kiss my ass.

The third was that my pride is worth exactly $6.40.

These, like all poker lessons, did not come easy or cheap. Actually, the last one came pretty cheap.

**I embarked on my new life** as a fledgling professional poker player determined to be smart. I stifled my true nature as a daydreamer and procrastinator. I resisted giving myself a colorful nickname like "the Predator," "the Mind Reader," or "Frisco Pat." I fought the urge to go to the local jeweler to get sized for a pinky ring or a trophy bracelet.

If I was going to win the World Series, or even become a winning player at any level, I would have to erase all my bad gambling habits and begin anew, learning the game and its strategies from the ground up. I decided to learn everything I could about poker before betting another dime in a game. It is said that any long journey begins with a single step, but in my experience it usually begins with a trip to the mall. Believing that the solutions to all life's mysteries can be found on the printed page, I hit my local bookstore. Entering a supersized book warehouse is an intimidating act for any writer. There are hundreds of millions of words in print surrounded by crowds only interested in buying discount cat calendars. If I felt bad walking through the stacks, I felt worse when I found my way to the Games section. Hundreds of poker books lined the shelves—titles on every conceivable variation of the game, biographies of famous players, and many personal narratives. Thankfully, I soon found that all the books were written by people who had some reputation or skill, so I was safe. There were no books written by ignorant pretenders. I thanked my stars I hadn't decided to write a book about politics, where being a know-nothing jackass is credential enough.

I pulled them from the stacks one by one, making a pile that grew above my waist. Generally, the books can be divided into three categories, with most falling into the how-to type. From these, I picked *Play Poker Like the Pros* by Phil Hellmuth, *Tournament Poker* by Tom McEvoy, *Poker Night* by John Vorhaus, *Shuffle Up and Deal* by Mike Sexton, *The Theory of Poker* by David Sklansky, and, of course, *Super System* by Doyle Brunson, and many other titles.

The second category covers memoirs and anecdotal compilations. I pulled out *Positively Fifth Street*, *Total Poker*, *The Biggest Game in Town*, *The Hand I Played*, *The Education of a Poker Player*, *Telling Lies and Getting Paid*, *Bad Beats and Lucky Draws*, and *Poker Nation*, to name a few. I really don't know where these guys find time to play, because they seem to spend all their time writing.

Finally, there are the tidbit books chock-full of ancillary information designed to hone your game. I chose *Caro's Book of Poker Tells* and *Caro's Fundamental Secrets of Winning Poker*, *The*

*Championship Table at the World Series of Poker, Poker Tournament Tips from the Pros* and *52 Tips for Texas Hold 'em Poker, Winning Methods of Bluffing & Betting in Poker,* and *77 Ways to Get the Edge at Casino Poker.*

After the first cut, I had a pile of forty books. I tried to put some back. Which books did I not need? *Poker Wisdom of a Champion?* I certainly needed that. Did I need *Poker: A Winner's Guide* or *The Winner's Guide to Hold 'em?* Better get the pair. How about *Championship No-Limit and Pot-Limit Hold 'Em?* That sounded perfect. Should I buy *Basic Poker* or *Tournament Poker for Advanced Players?* Both, of course.

Trying to cull the herd was taking too long, and some punk kid kept asking me if I needed any help. The third time he came around, his query had lost any pretense of customer service, and when he used the word *sir,* it was clear he meant *dickhead.* Squatting on the floor behind several towers of books, I must have looked like a kid building a fort. I asked him if he knew which of these books were exceptionally good. *Poker for Dummies,* he told me, *is a good place to start.* I was paralyzed by indecision, but poker is all about making good decisions. So I looked at the stack fiercely and vowed to pick three titles and come back for more if I needed them. I tried to use the same system I have for buying wine and hair gel: The more expensive it is, the better it is. Every book, however, was overpriced. A quarter-inch-thick paperback was $19.95. Every eighth of an inch of thickness cost five bucks more. A favorite price point for poker publishers seems to be $29.95. I put back a few books, but then I began to worry that I would pick the wrong books and set myself on a course bound for failure. If I got at least one valuable skill from each book, they would pay for themselves quickly. I picked up a stack that weighed about five pounds and cost around $400.

*I'll take these,* I told the punk.

*All of them, sir?* This time he said *sir* in a manner that told me he worked on commission.

*Yeah. And I need them individually gift-wrapped.*

*Of course, sir,* he said, back to meaning *dickhead.*

I now had a stack of poker books, a $400 credit-card bill, and some bitter memories of snide and bemused bookstore flunkies. But I was charged. For two days straight I read every word on No-Limit Hold 'em and everything I could find on tournament tactics. I took notes, flagged pages, and boldly underlined. I was enthralled by the complex strategies and thoughtful theories relayed by men of disparate backgrounds who had left the world of neckties and paychecks to play cards day and night, and I was proud to be joining their ranks, even if only in a half-assed manner. I pored over detailed accounts of famous games and convinced myself that I would make the same brilliant moves or avoid the same blunders as the pros.

Heeding the advice of the first book I read, I bought a ledger to keep track of my winnings and losses and opened a checking account just for my poker career. I scoured the appendixes for the best poker software and ordered it shipped overnight. I went to online poker sites and registered under the alias "the editor." Through some fancy feature on my cell phone, I even downloaded two Texas Hold 'em games, one for $6.49 and the other for $7.49, so I could play on the train and during meetings.

What I found was that all the books have different philosophies but the same standard rules of law. These tenets are no secret and are clearly stated in almost every book about playing poker. Many times they are even followed by exclamation points, which poker writers have a particular affinity for.

The secrets to being a championship-caliber no-limit high-stakes pro are as follows:

1. Choose your starting hands carefully.

When you are dealt the cards, you have the option of calling the minimum bet, raising it, or folding your hand. If you decide to play, make sure your cards are good or have the potential to become something powerful. Otherwise, fold and enjoy the fine casino air and watch the other players pick their teeth with their pinky nails.

2. Play position.

Where you are sitting relative to the dealer button is very important. The dealer gets to act last, so he knows what every other player is going to do before him. The dealer is the last word in the hand. The poor schmuck to his left is the first to act, so he has to make his decisions while not knowing what anyone else will do.

3. Read your opponents' tells.

People have little tics and habits that can betray how nervous or excited they are, and if you are observant, you can pick up on these. For example, if someone peeks at his cards and sits straight up, pumps his fist, and shouts, *Aces!*, he might have a good hand. He could also just be a lunatic.

4. Hide your own tells.

Everyone has at least one tell. I tend to turn bright red, suddenly flop sweat, and become paralyzed when I have a good hand. When I'm bluffing, I turn as white as Tip O'Neill's inner thigh, tremble violently, and become incontinent. To combat these subtleties, I wear sunglasses, a plastic bag over my head, and Depends.

5. Capitalize on your opponents' mistakes.

People make mistakes all the time. I, for one, make one about every minute and a half. When you think someone's making a mistake, find a way to translate that into personal profit for you. And not just in poker; do it in life too, like Gandhi.

6. Manage your bankroll.

Tracking your winnings and losses is a vital poker skill. I will track my winnings carefully, but I will turn a blind eye to my losses because that is just depressing. Winnings are profit; losses are just one-time costs that are actually investments in winning. I learned that from Enron.

7. Don't go on tilt.

Tilting is losing your bearings because of doing something wrong or having some bad luck come your way. It's just poker jargon for being pissed off. I'm in pretty good shape with this rule because I've been on tilt since October 22, 1978, for reasons I'd rather not get into, so I'm used to it.

8. Calculate the odds.

This has something to do with math.

9. Make good decisions.

You can't control the cards, but you can control what you do with them. Everything in poker is about making the right decision at the right time. How hard can that be? I've made a few bad decisions, granted. Wearing that MUSTACHES ARE EFFETE T-shirt to the policemen's ball comes to mind, but when the time comes to make the big choices, I'll know what to do.

10. Be lucky.

Every player talks about the luck factor, particularly in large tournaments. I just have to hope that, when the time comes, luck will shine its juicy rays down upon me. I haven't won the lottery yet or found a large amount of money. Sure, I'm healthy and have a beautiful wife and son, but the purely fiscal branch of luck has been historically derelict in rewarding me. So I'm due.

All I had to do was learn these tenets and incorporate them into my game and I'd be a winner. I might not have every slick move down, but I could beat the herds of donkeys that filled the tables. Ten rules can be tricky to remember and prioritize in all situations, but, fortunately, the books seemed to agree that a policy of selective aggression complements all points well. My home game was the first time I played like I meant it, and I used all the rules as best I could, and, surprising even to me, everything went according to plan. I didn't know it at the time, but I was playing selective/aggressive.

Selective/aggressive strategy simply means that you should be very choosy with the hand and the table position you decide to enter the pot with and bet assertively. Could it be that simple? After forty-eight hours of reading, I felt ready to ditch the training and jump into the high-stakes table with the deed to my house.

The idea of going into a casino card room, however, is intimidating if you've never done it. Late-night cable has plenty of commercials for my local club. If you were to believe the image as seen on TV, everyone at the card club is smiling, laughing, and winning. I had occasion one afternoon to walk through the club, just out of curiosity, and I wasn't buying. A card room is full of, to paraphrase what George Carlin said about kids, a few winners and a whole lot of losers. It's a mean place, by design, full of cold, hungry people looking for fresh meat. I wasn't going there until I was ready, and that wasn't just yet.

Instead, I turned my attention to my new cell-phone game, which started me at a fictional table in an imaginary Indian casino against four "players." If you beat everyone at the table, you advance to a riverboat, then Atlantic City, and then a Caribbean resort. If you beat every table, you go to the championship table. This game took about two minutes to download into my phone, so the programming couldn't be very sophisticated. Still, I couldn't seem to get past the first table. Every time I had a pair, someone had a higher pair. If I tried to bluff, everyone called me. If I had aces, everyone folded. I dismissed all this as an anomaly. It wasn't real poker. Still, it was vexing to lose twenty matches in a row against my own phone. *Vexing* might not be the right word, but my thesaurus lacks a synonym for *completely fucking humiliating*.

Then the poker software showed up in the mailbox.

Playing a computer program is to poker what masturbation is to sex. No one, rightfully, is even slightly impressed if you're successful. Just as it lacks any impressive lasting thrill, however, it is also devoid of the pressure going to a card club might produce, and once you've purchased a game, it costs nothing to play. So I slugged in the disk and loaded it onto my computer. It took a few minutes for me to realize that I'd bought the Limit Texas Hold 'em version. *No matter,* I thought, *if I can play no-limit well, I'll beat limit no problem.*

After fooling around awhile with the game's features, I was asked by the computer if I would be interested in challenging Mike, the computer's poker pro persona, who is given the same one hundred hands of Hold 'em as you are to play against other fictional players. At the end of the challenge, your earnings or losses are compared to Mike's. I took this challenge gleefully, knowing a program routine could not outplay me, armed as I was with my new poker wisdom.

I began to play and was doing fine. I was playing a lot of hands and getting lucky on the flop. I really wished I was playing for cash. After fifty hands, a box popped up on my screen informing me that halfway through the game, I was indeed beating Mike, which, given my confidence level, was not much of a surprise. But my cards began to dry up. I got nothing playable at all, so I began bluffing more often. My virtual opponents were not intimidated, nor did they care that I had four hundred clams' worth of poker wisdom on my desk. After losing a couple of big hands and getting outdrawn, I was down. When one hundred hands were over, the pop-up told me that I was negative $834. Mike, however, was up $19, playing the same hands against the same number of opponents. What crap. This had to be wrong. Sure, I made a few mistakes, but there is no way that I could have played differently to the extent that I would win instead of lose. Thankfully, the program had the option of replaying the same sessions, so once more unto the breach, dear friends . . . I lost again and again. I did manage to lose less, mostly by staying out of hands I remembered to be bad for my bankroll. Mike meanwhile continued to win. He, or rather it, kept winning, and I kept losing. Sometimes I'd win and he'd win more or I'd lose and he'd lose less.

I decided the game was cheating, or at least fundamentally flawed. It's the poor workman who blames his tools, however, so I poked around the game's features a bit more. I discovered that the computer generated hundreds of player types of varying skill levels and styles. The game was also designed with plenty of analytic tools that allowed me to see what I was doing wrong. After every game, I could look at statistics and learn what mistakes I was making over time. If I click on the advice button, a screen comes up that lays out all the odds and the computer's recommendation on whether to fold, raise, or call based on the way the other players are betting. It's a wealth of information; the only problem is that I hate it.

In a nutshell, the computer's advice seemed a little repetitive: fold, fold, fold, fold, fold. Call, then fold. Fold, fold, fold, fold, fold, fold, fold, fold, fold, fold, fold, fold, fold. Raise, then fold. Fold, fold, fold, and fold. I played for hours and wished I was somewhere else doing something more exciting, like stuffing envelopes at the DMV.

The best I can tell, the way to play limit poker is to not play. You sit and wait, deferring to everyone else until you finally get a hand and everyone defers to you. If, like I did when the tedium began to eat at me like rust, you decide to take some risk and play, nobody ever folds because they all have something. If they have something good, they call; if they have something great, they raise. If you have a great hand and they have a good hand, they just call your bets and you make a small amount of money. You can't bluff because someone always calls you. Limit poker is for guys trying to kill time before they die. The game is flawed and that's why I lost. That's my story and I'm sticking to it.

By now, the online gaming sites had received my checks and I was ready to play. Under my moniker, "the editor," I cruised around the sites familiarizing myself with the virtual landscape. It was glorious. Hundreds of poker games and tournaments were going on with stakes as high as $400 and $800 blinds down to 1¢ and 2¢.

To get my feet wet, I started at the free tables. I was given $1,000 in valueless chips, and I found a seat at a $10/$20 game. After just a few seconds of familiarizing myself, I started playing. And it was great. I won and won. The other players were horrible, either completely reckless or so tight they folded to any raise. I busted out three players in ten minutes. They didn't care much, it seemed, because the computer refilled your chip stack whenever you went broke. In half an hour, I had ten grand in chips, and I left the table seeking greater fortune. At a higher-stakes table, I continued my run and doubled up three times. I suffered a few beats and got chased out of some pots, but overall I was tearing up the joint. I moved up the stakes ladder again and again.

In just a few hours, I turned one thousand phony chips into more than a half million. I was so proud of myself that I dragged my wife into the room to look at my inflated fake account. *Wow!* she gushed. *Now you can buy a pretend Ferrari.* My wife saves her praise for actual accomplishments and not the world of make-believe.

I was undaunted. If I could run my stake up 500 percent on the free tables, then, even if the cash players were ten times as good as the free rollers, I'd still do very well. My line of logic seemed flawless. It occurred to me that I was wasting my time playing for free, especially when I was on a rush.

I openly entertained the idea that I could start playing seriously for low stakes and escalate my game all the way to the world championship. I'd played some tough games, I figured, and if I got a lot of practice playing below my level, I would move up steadily and profitably. Hell, I might even become world champion having invested only a buck or two.

*Playing for money should always be taken seriously,* I told myself as I joined a 1¢/2¢ game and brought in $2 from my account. Ten seconds later, I was calling a big bet, 10¢, with lousy cards. Why? Because it was 10¢. Who cared about 10¢? My opponent got lucky on the flop, but not as lucky as me. He moved all-in and I called. His three of a kind failed to impress my straight, and I busted him.

And so it went for a couple of nights, as I played for pittance stakes after work when my wife and son were asleep. I began to suffer a few beats here and there, but I was still up. I made the decision to make the jump to a 5¢/10¢ game. It was a little tougher, but people still folded to my aggressive play. I didn't care about this amount of money either, so I had no fear. Then things changed.

I began to lose. My aggression seemed to backfire, my long-shot cards didn't come through, and my bluffs were called. When I did have a hand, it was the second best. My first losing night, I was down $1. The next night, I lost $10. Three more bad nights left only $6.40 in my account, and, feeling baffled, I slinked back down to the 1¢/2¢ game. I hoped to build back my stack and, more important, my confidence, and continue my march toward glory.

Everything started fine and I won some nice pots and had ten bucks in front of me. Then Mr. Fish joined the game, and a few hands later I was broke.

Playing online has certain advantages, like not having to leave the house. It has difficulties too, like not getting to leave the house. There are no cocktail waitresses either, and I really could have used a stiff drink. Instead, I went to bed a broke, sober loser.

After lying in bed cursing Mr. Fish and the game of poker, I started going over in my mind the many hands that had cleaned me out. There were certainly a few bad beats, not the least of which was the last one, and I could remember every detail of these plays. When I added up the losses from these suck-outs and million-to-one shots, it only totaled one-quarter of what I had lost.

What the hell happened to the rest? I lost a bunch of hands betting on small pairs that didn't improve. My suited connectors that didn't connect to anything but each other cost me some dough when I stuck with them for the turn and the river. Playing a pair of jacks or tens when there were higher cards on the board cost me plenty. Bluffing with nothing at all could have gone a lot better.

During my mental autopsy, it began to register that I was in so many hands I couldn't possibly remember most of them specifically. Eureka. Why was I in so many hands? Because I was playing almost every hand, at least to the flop. Most times I would fold to a bet if I had nothing or, worse, hang on if there was even a remote chance of getting something. If I played a four and three of clubs and a three came on the flop, I would call bets even if there was an ace or a king beside my little trey hoping for more. I had a lot of fun when it worked, but that was only a couple of times out of dozens.

Most times, I'd done well with the aggressive part of my strategy: betting and putting pressure on my opponent to fold his better hand. The more I did this, the more the other players began to doubt the quality of my hole cards, so they would raise me back. I'd fold or call and lose.

The way you want to play poker is the way you want to play golf: fewer but better strokes than the other guys. The best player is the one who doesn't break a sweat or find himself picking burrs out of his socks after shooting from the rough. How brilliantly you play from the sand doesn't matter compared to avoiding it altogether.

To torture another sports analogy, if you're the toughest guy in the world and you use your aggression selectively—in the boxing ring—you're going to be rich and famous. If you are not selective about where you use your aggression, you're going to wind up in jail or dead.

The most screwed-up part of this epiphany was that I knew all this beforehand. The more you sit out hands, the more your play will get respect when you do enter a pot. You can't sit them all out waiting for aces or you are not going to make any money and the blinds will eat away at your stack, but you have to have something most every time you play. I knew all this, even before reading the books. What screwed me up was winning while playing badly. I'd gotten it in my head that not only was I a better player than the nickel-and-dimers around me, but I could also win consistently without the benefit of having decent cards. Fucking hubris again.

There's nothing like starting a poker career by busting out. My online poker career began with playing the free tables, where nothing real is risked and nothing real is gained. You play with fake dollars provided by the host company, and when you lose them, they're instantly replenished. Ostensibly, this service exists to prepare you for the real cash tables, but in reality it only serves to make you into a chump. When there is nothing real to lose, there is no aversion to risk. So everyone calls and raises with little regard to the quality of their own hands or the actions of other players. Playing poker for real money, I'm now aware, is nothing like this.

I couldn't be mad at Mr. Fish. The next time we played, I was going to compliment him on his good play. I would respect his game and see if there was anything I could learn from watching him. Then I would empty his piggy bank.

**I met Betsy,** as I'll call her, at some boring industry shindig, where people in publishing were supposed to network and build a community. In actuality, it was mostly a bunch of wannabes and interns looking for paying jobs. I went for the free drinks and the chance to suck up to some book reviewers. Another editor introduced me to Betsy, a local wheeler-dealer whose name appears regularly in newspaper columns chronicling charity and art stuff I have little interest in.

If her wardrobe and jewelry were any indication, Betsy worked for reasons having nothing to do with needing a paycheck. She was, nonetheless, charming and engaging, and asked many pointed questions, although I was sure she couldn't possibly give a rat's ass. I knew from the society page that she had just gotten married in the spate of gay nuptials that followed the mayor of San Francisco's issuing licenses to same-sex couples, and I congratulated her. She thanked me warmly and gave me her card, signaling to me that my time was up. As her interest in me waned, I made, by chance, an offhand comment that I was writing a book on poker.

Betsy told me she had recently begun hosting a game for friends, but she only knew the game from television, where information on etiquette was sorely lacking. Would I be interested in joining them and giving her some guidance? My interest in poker suddenly made me an expert in her eyes. I was flattered, and I immediately confirmed my assistance and attendance. A game full of well-heeled swells, loaded with cash but lacking experience or even fundamental skills? A dream come true to a budding pro like me. This opportunity would be great for the book and, if I didn't blow it, would be a boon for my poker fund. I'd played in a few home games recently and lost money at every one. My bankroll had been completely wiped out twice and had to be replenished. I made mistakes that I knew to be stupid, like drinking during the games and soft-playing friends who were short-stacked. I vowed to stay sober and play hard-core this time, taking no prisoners and offering no apologies.

**Good to her boss's word,** Betsy's assistant called a few days later with a bunch of questions about poker protocol and procedures, which I either knew or made up in a believable fashion. The next week an invitation arrived at my office with the time and the date.

I was excited to play, but I wanted to be smart. Many poker books advise developing a plan before entering a tournament. I decided to treat Betsy's game like a tournament and work up a solid strategy. I didn't know any of the players, but I guessed they were mostly beginners and dilettantes.

Much of my plan would depend on my table image. Table image is how the others perceive your style. Some players play very few hands, and when they do, they have only premium hands, like aces, kings, or suited ace/king. They don't bluff and rarely bet large amounts. They're called tight players or rocks. Calling stations are players who call a lot of bets and often fold if the action gets too high. Both these types of players are easy to bluff. Maniacs call and raise with speculative hands or nothing at all. They can't be bluffed. A solid player is someone who makes decisions based on good information and mathematical probabilities and rarely makes spectacular mistakes.

There are times when table image is more important than your cards. At the final table of the World Series of Poker in 2004, Josh Arieh, a very aggressive pro, bet with a respectable suited ace/jack in the best position, the dealer's spot. But Dan Harrington, known as a very tight but solid aggressive player, raised from the big blind, the worst position. Arieh knew that Harrington's raise meant that all their chips could be in the pot by the time the river came, and if he didn't want to risk all his chips with his ace/jack, he should fold now. Dan Harrington had a ten/four offsuit.

Author Mike "the Mad Genius of Poker" Caro is a master of table image. He wears disheveled clothes and his hair splays out from his scalp like he is holding one of those static electricity orbs found in children's museums. His expressions are exaggerated and his gestures are over the top. He never shuts up, asking other players strange questions and going off on tangents having nothing to do with poker. He looks like a maniac, but he plays very tight. Other players are so aware of him, they assume he's in every hand, but his activities are strictly theatrical. He patiently waits for good cards, and when he has a hand, he gets a lot of action from people who think he's insane or just want to get him out of the game.

If Betsy told the other players I was a poker writer, I might be given credit for being some sort of poker specialist. Most players would probably avoid me in the beginning of the game and, after they felt more comfortable and daring, come after me at the end. I'd play loose/aggressive early and tighten up toward the end.

Another option was that I could protest or deny any expertise—that is to say, tell the truth. I could play a lot of hands and get caught bluffing a few times. This would tell everyone that I'm a very loose player who bets without good cards. I would get a lot of action after I switched gears. *Switching gears* is slang for altering your poker style to throw off your opponents. I could start loose and then go tight and clean up. Either way I decided to go, it was another flawless plan.

**If you've never been** a guest at someone's house where the driveway can accommodate more than a dozen cars, then I feel sorry for your poor ass. When I got there, I didn't know what to expect. I knew no one and was far from familiar shores. After a brief hello, I was abandoned by the busy host, who scooted into the kitchen. A few early and well-acquainted guests were huddled by a wet bar having an animated discussion. Betsy was in the kitchen, and I was standing next to an ugly statue at the door without my shoes.

Luckily, I'd been tipped off about the shoe issue. The carpets were white, so everyone was expected to remove their shoes and place them in a spacious rack near the portico. Knowing this ahead of time, I was spared the worry that my socks were mismatched, in tatters, or menacingly ripe. The smell of my socks, my wife likes to say, can knock a buzzard off a shit wagon.

I was meandering about pretending to look at the art when a man came out of the kitchen carrying a tray of hors d'oeuvres and cold cuts. As he set up a spread on a sideboard, I realized I'd gone to high school with him. We caught up for a bit, and he told me he had a catering business. I couldn't remember his name and he couldn't remember mine, but we both pretended otherwise. I asked if he handled a lot of poker parties, and he said he did at least two a week and that there were more calls all the time. He set me straight on the difference between endive and radicchio, a distinction I'd never bothered to figure out.

Since he was only dropping off the food, he excused himself, and I was alone again with my make-believe art study. More guests had arrived and joined the coven by the bar. They were all women. I shouldn't have been so surprised, as I assumed a lesbian woman would have lesbian friends. These ones were exactly as I'd expected—well-heeled, professional couples, who, like the host, were there to celebrate the newest cool thing, having moved past cigars, book clubs, and wine tasting. The thing about rich, well-educated Northern Californians is that they go the extra mile to appear earthy and practical. There's really no point in being rich if you can't pretend you're a struggling artist. Perhaps this is because, in the Bay Area, struggling artists are higher on the social ladder than the merely prosperous. Another man did show up, but he sat behind his wife to learn the game while simultaneously criticizing her play.

I needed a drink. Screw the sober part of my plan; I could still take down the game with a few beers in me. At the wet bar, a woman asked if I'd like a glass of wine. I said yes, despite my distaste for wine other than champagne. I have certain refined tastes, but I generally like to drink only beer, because no matter what the libation, I drink the same amount of liquid regardless of the alcohol content. (If I had my druthers, I'd drink only straight, ice-cold gin, but I'd certainly have no wife, no child, no job, no cognitive functions, and, most days, no pants.) From the suburbs of the crowd, I listened for a moment, hoping everyone was discussing the upcoming game so I could get an early sense of each woman's experience. But the other imbibers were just cooing about their last trip to the Burgundy region of France. I excused myself in a way to suggest having a weak bladder or to be in desperate need of cheese.

I wanted a beer, a liquid devoid of complexity, without hints of any fragrance normally reserved for potpourri bowls. So I downed my wine in a single gulp and reached around the bar for a Beck's and stepped out on the porch for a cigarette, assuming that I couldn't smoke inside. Smoking inside is an anachronism in California. You can't smoke in restaurants, bars, casinos, or massage parlors. You can't smoke at the race track if there's anything above your head other than blue sky. On Betsy's deck, thank God, there was a nice standing ashtray, so I assumed she had little problem with smokers. I was joined outside by a youngish black couple, both with dreadlocks, but one was very tall and one fairly short. The short woman had really brilliant white teeth. They introduced themselves and we chatted about our respective relationships with the host and other banalities. For reasons beyond understanding, when the conversation hit a lull, I blurted out, *You have really nice teeth.*

Their polite smiles froze and they exchanged a glance. I was stricken with the horror that I had touched on a stereotype of which I was previously unaware. But the woman, whose name had been purged from my memory by my panic, said thank you and continued on with the banter. I lit another butt and pretended to admire the view. I was relieved when they excused themselves and went back in.

I was beginning to get anxious about whether the game was actually going to happen, fearing that the collective guests had silently decided to screw the poker game and instead make a night of chitchatting about good restaurants and bad U.S. foreign policy. On cue, through the sliding glass doors I saw Betsy walk out of the kitchen and direct everyone over to the poker table, already set up and appointed with chips and coasters. Her game was going to start on time, she said, even though it was now one hour and forty-five minutes late. I took a last drag and snuffed the cigarette out in the fancy ashtray. Betsy saw me, opened the door, and said, *Dear, please don't put that out in my bird feeder.*

**Finally at the table,** I wondered if I could create a successful table image from being a shoeless, racist bird-hater. Betsy presented me since I was the only new person there. Ten introductions in ten seconds probably isn't a world record in Betsy's world, but it was the equivalent of a shock-and-awe attack in mine. I remembered no names at the end of it, and, to make matters worse, everyone remembered mine. I was presented as "the poker player," with the sly implication that I was the one who was expected to take everyone's money and, in exchange for that, answer all their questions. A hippieish woman asked how I did at the last World Series of Poker. I was inspired to say I had broken even, not mentioning, of course, that I only watched it on television.

Betsy now seemed eager to get started, saying she had yoga at dawn and wanted to be in bed by eleven o'clock. It was a quarter past nine. I couldn't wait for any hands with this time limit, but neither could anyone else. Having no knowledge of any player's good or bad habits, I took the seat nearest the bathroom.

I had played poker with female players before, but never exclusively female players. Most pros, when asked, say women make better players overall because of their ability to read cards. They could just be trying to be politically correct or they could be telling the truth. Most men I've seen at the poker table have been fairly dismissive of women players, often to their own peril.

During the finals of the 2003 Ladies Night tourney, it was the supple blonde Clonie Gowan versus the kittenish Evelyn Ng. When Clonie won a big pot, the almost all-male audience burst into applause. I thought Clonie must be the crowd favorite until Evelyn took down a big pile and the same men burst into applause. The men in the audience didn't seem to care who won because this was their ultimate fantasy—a catfight on the poker table. This is sad because they played great poker. Every play was mistake free. Both women made great reads, aggressive bets, and, hardest of all, tough laydowns. I'd have to say it was the best final table I've ever seen televised.

I have seen enough of my money go into women's stacks to expunge any misconceptions about gender making a bit of difference when it comes to poker abilities.

**Everyone gave Besty** a hundred bucks except for the woman to whom the host owed money for some floral arrangements and the woman who I learned was Betsy's spouse and who clearly wanted Betsy to take care of it for her. After a few words of welcome and the buying-in routine, everyone was offered a cheat sheet explaining the hierarchy of hands. I was able to note who took one for constant reference and who just peeked at it to see if a straight beat a flush or vice versa. Immediately, I picked up a lot of helpful information: who was an out-and-out neophyte, who was as rusty at cards as I was at social etiquette.

The first hand played in a home game can set the mood for the whole game. All the poker books say people play tight in the beginning, and if you are going to size up someone's play, you have to wait an hour or so while self-discipline fades and a gambler's true game rises up. I didn't have time for that, and, besides, I've found it is not at all true for home games. In the home game, everyone has gotten their babysitters and found parking. They have a few drinks and they are among friends. They don't want to fold a hundred times waiting for a decent pair. They've come to play their cards, and, most of the time, expect to lose.

I like winning the first hand in a home game, particularly on a bluff, because it's the only hand people play timidly. If at all possible, I go all-in on the first hand. Everyone folds because, while they all want to play the opening hand, absolutely no one wants to lose all their money three minutes into the game. When I take the pot, I show my, hopefully, crappy cards and listen to everyone moan. Then I tighten up and only play good hands or try to see flops cheap or for free.

The first hand was dealt, and I watched the other players looking at their cards, hoping to establish a kind of behavioral baseline. I wanted to see if they would cover their cards up, lose interest immediately, or sit up excitedly. I hoped also to see who would bet wildly and who would call the most bets and fold after the flop. Information is everywhere at the table. The trouble isn't finding data but discerning what is relevant and what is just random noise.

I hoped to see a bunch of wild betting, and I wasn't

disappointed. From under the gun, a woman named, I think, Kathy raised the pot confidently. The woman on her left, Theresa, looked at her cards and immediately reraised. The others folded in turn as the table became silent. I peeked at my cards for three seconds, then placed them neatly down and put a few chips on top to protect them from wind and cheaters. I glanced at my chips and the chips in the pot. I leaned back in my chair and put a hand on my hip. This body language is classic for someone with big cards. Even to those who don't know poker tells, this is a subconscious projection of confidence, and I played it nicely. I looked solemnly across the table to the pair of bettors to see how worried they looked. They didn't look happy, but that wasn't good news. They were looking at each other and only at each other. They missed my performance entirely. It took me a moment to grasp the situation. These two were not friends; they were a couple.

When one friend goes over the top of another friend, the tension can rise. When someone does it to their spouse, it reaches another level entirely. Kathy stared at her partner, not sizing her up but glaring her down, as if the reraise was an insult that should either be immediately retracted or, if it could not be withdrawn, would come with serious consequences. The action was back to Kathy, and she took a long eight seconds to glower at her life partner with a look I knew well. It said:

*You selfish, insensitive jerk.*

*You just had to step all over me to make yourself look good.*

*How could you do this?*

*There's going to be hell to pay now.*

*You know that thing you like me to do to you that I don't like doing but do anyway just to make you happy?*

*I am never doing that thing again.*

The bettor's face flashed the standard array of responses in perfect order, from amusement through bafflement and stoicism, and finally to umbrage:

*Ha! I got you.*

*What? Why are you mad?*
*I didn't do anything wrong, did I?*
*No I didn't. I'm allowed to be myself.*
*Stop making a scene.*
*You're mad at me?*
*Well, now I'm madder than you. Go to hell.*

I have had this nonverbal argument many times from both positions, and I knew it was going to last all night. This type of melee gets worked out alone, after the standard period of angry silence. But that wasn't my concern. Neither one was going to fold this hand as long as the other one was in it. Unless I had a pair of aces, I was going to fold. Moreover, I vowed to stay out of every pot that the couple was in all night unless I had the absolute nuts.

For a moment, the scene threatened to move from seething silence to the arena of the very much out loud, but both parties mutely decided to settle this in the car after the game. I folded, a ten/nine offsuit, as did the few players behind me. The women had their showdown, with Theresa, the reraiser, beating Kathy with a pair of tens versus ace high.

The chitchat resumed and so did the game. I kept looking for a spot to make a play but had little success. I noticed that a woman named Donna, on my left, always raised when Beth, the woman with the white teeth, brought in a bet. They never actually spoke to each other and clearly were not a couple, but they might have been together in the past. I couldn't get a read on their cards because they were not really playing their cards, and their bets were so large relative to the pot size, I had to fold. When I had a good hand, no one gave me any action. When the twisted sisters were firing shells at each other, I had crap hands. I didn't bring more than $100 and couldn't buy back in if I was beat. The troublemakers went broke every few hands and bought more chips. They would trade chips with their adversaries but not with the rest of the table, and especially not with me.

My plan to run the table by making aggressive bets and

projecting an intimidating table image was being thwarted by emotional relationships having nothing to do with poker. You can't terrorize someone who doesn't even know you exist. You can't bluff someone who will not fold. You cannot call big bets with weak cards.

A few of the players who had no conflicts and I played straight up for a few pots, but mostly we stayed out of the drama queens' way. Betsy soon called the last round, and I finally caught a real hand, a pair of red kings. I was down from the blinds and having my calls and small raises bullied by bigger bets. I was going to win this pot or grab the ugly statue next to the front door and fence it. One way or another, I was going to leave this nuthouse a winner.

All four firebrands came in raising. I raised my last meager chips all-in and caught a few stiff glances for my trouble. They were used to me and everyone else staying out of the way. They all called. A pot was established consisting of all my chips and an equal amount from each of them and the blinds. You cannot win more than your own maximum bet multiplied by the number of callers. This was all I could win. The four of them continued to bet in a side pot to decide, I guess, who was right and who was wrong.

My kings took my pot, and when I cashed out I had just a few dollars more than I had started with. Given how the evening had gone, I considered this an extraordinary and unexpected victory. I said my good-byes and lied about coming back next time and gave that statue a passing glance and got the hell out of there.

Driving home, I felt pretty proud of myself for winning a big hand at the end and recovering a bunch of chips. The more I thought about it, though, the more I realized I had played like a fool again. I deferred to the table image of others, believing that their recklessness was dangerous to me. They brought their real life to the table, and I didn't take advantage of it. Anytime someone is making decisions based on anything other than solid hands and pot odds, there is a way to make them pay for it. Any pro would have wiped that game up, and I barely survived. I let other players dictate my actions.

The reason I lost a fortune, relatively speaking, playing for pennies is because too many times when I had the best cards, I folded, and when I had the second-best cards, I stayed in. This was by design. Not by my design, but by theirs. My opponents took action to make me fold or make me stay in, depending on what was best for them. This time, however, the circumstances were different. The actions of the other players were taken with little or no regard for me, but the effect was the same—losing.

*What should I have done differently?*

This is the question that haunts poker players and occasionally drives them mad. Every serious player asks himself that question after every tournament, every game, and, sometimes, every hand. This is how you get better. If the honest answer is, *Exactly what you did do, it was just bad luck,* then that player can sleep soundly that night. This is, however, rarely the answer. This game was screwed up for me from the outset, but what options did I have to mitigate the circumstances? What did I miss?

What should I have done differently? Should I have called large bets with less than premium hands? That would have been stupid. Should I have made large bets when I was the first to act? That was wild play, too. Normally, I would have brushed off the game as an anomaly. I had already dismissed my losses online and with the computer game as exceptions. I was making excuses for myself and getting sick of it. So what should I have done differently—specifically? Thinking back, I remember that a couple of times someone raised the pot after Donna had bet but before Beth could fire back. This seemed excuse enough for Beth to fold her hand. Beth wanted to beat Donna but did not want to go broke to a third party. With her nemesis out of the hand, Donna usually played weaker and would fold marginal hands. I could have been the person making those in-between raises, and made some nice pots.

Kathy and Theresa were trickier. Neither seemed to care if

someone else was in their pot, but there was an opening there as well. On the few occasions when Theresa didn't play back, Kathy tended to lose interest in her hand and would either call bets from other players with medium hands or fold weak hands. If she had a real hand, she would go all-in. It might have cost me a bit betting at her alone, but the amount of money I would have gotten from her laydowns would have been a tidy sum. I could have pulled this move at least a half-dozen times.

My table image, which I had put most of my stock in, had become weak because my play was weak. It does not matter how much you look the part if you don't act to back it up. Seeming smart won't play if you act stupidly, and trying to intimidate other players by folding won't work either. The action drives the image, not the other way around.

My biggest sin, however, was that I did not read the table or the players effectively. I noticed the relationships between the other players and concluded that they influenced their play, but I did not find a way to use that to my advantage. Instead, I used it as an excuse to play weakly. If I had deconstructed the players' betting habits and found a way to pressure them into folding or trap them into calling and raising, I could have cleaned the game up completely. With every hand I watched, I should have been able to gain insight into each player and use it for my benefit. I should have put each player on a hand—meaning to guess what they had—and compared my speculation to their actual hand when they had to turn up their cards. If I was right, I would win; if I was wrong, I could adjust my deductive criteria and try again. I have never had the preternatural ability to instantaneously read cards. Phil "Poker Brat" Hellmuth is a master at this. If you have ever seen him act as a commentator during a poker tournament, it is amazing. A player will make a bet, the same size bet he's made a dozen times before, and Phil will say, "I think he has a pair of queens," and sure enough, he does. I doubt I will ever be that good, but if I pay attention, I have a fair likelihood of determining who has a strong hand, a draw, or a stone-cold bluff. A good player is in every hand even if his cards aren't.

Eventually, you can get a sense of who likes to raise early with speculative hands and who likes to wait for big pairs or who likes to call with weak cards or slow-play big ones. A good player can deconstruct an entire table's action before it is his turn to bet. Then he can make a decision confidently.

If I was such a genius, why was I making this brilliant analysis here and now, in my car, driving home with my $3 profit and approaching the $5 tollbooth? Doing a bit of rough math, I came to the conclusion that acting on these small bits of observation would have doubled my buy-in and sent me home with an extra hundred bucks. That is not a lot of money, especially in poker, but it is a hell of a lot better than what I had now. And if I had made some bold moves, maybe the others would have rethought entering pots when I was yet to act. There was nothing inherently wrong in choosing the table image I did, but it was wrong to be so committed to one style that I could not adapt to the situation.

Being a day late and dollar short in poker skill is a perfect recipe for pain and suffering. The thought of improving my game enough to compete at a professional level was now even more daunting, which is to say it was impossible to even imagine. The time you have to gather information, process it, and act is mere seconds. I had left my house giddy with excitement and loudly predicting my certain win. I was going home a loser, again.

Making matters worse, I'd already told everyone I knew that I was writing a book about poker. *How's the poker book coming? How much have you won?* I kept getting asked. If someone asked me about the book right now, I'd say, *It's a disaster and I'm losing plenty. But enough about me. How are your genital warts? Any flare-ups lately?*

Was I just unlucky, which meant I would fail? Or was I just bad, in which case I would fail? Faced with two possibilities that are equally unappealing, I decided to reject the premise and redefine success. Hope and faith are great American traditions, more so to gamblers than to preachers.

I am capable of learning from my mistakes, and every lesson makes me a stronger player. Losing, I decided, was a part of learning. It was a good thing to do, at least early in the going. I would make the most of my losing now, so I could win later. Making mistakes is an important part of any process, and if you are smart, you will learn more from mistakes than from success. I would get better and I would win. I was going home and telling my wife the good news: I didn't win. And the next time someone asked me how the book was going, I would say, *Great. I'm losing.*

**The lessons** from the lesbians were still fresh in my mind the next evening as I was standing in the church basement holding a beer with one hand and shaking a priest's hand with the other. (If poker gives me nothing else, it's allowed me to write that sentence.) In the bowels of my local Catholic church I was watching what I suspected was an illegal poker tournament. Much as I wanted to, I was not playing . . . yet.

A family friend, J, had heard I liked poker and invited me to the game sponsored by the Men's Club of his local parish. Owing to the disorganization that comes from anything overseen by a committee, or my own incompetence, I had the wrong start time for the tournament. When I walked in the door half an hour early, I was half an hour late. I was crushed. I had felt slightly indulgent leaving my family at home and playing poker two nights in a row, but I couldn't pass up this game. When was I going to get a chance to play poker at church again?

J left the table he was playing at to say hello. He told me not to worry; they would put together a side game as soon as ten people got knocked out. There was nothing to do but observe, which was fine, because it really was something to see, or rather, hear. I got a beer, ate a sandwich, said hello to the padre, and wandered about for a while.

Eighty mostly portly men squeezed together against folding tables covered with felt swaths and topped with poker chips and beer cups is a common enough site in this great land of ours, but these fellas were loud. They talked loud, bet loud, and laughed loud. They yelled at each other across the room and across the table, they yelled at someone to bring them more beer, and they yelled at the cards. If I didn't know where I was, I would have guessed it was a tournament for deaf, overweight plumbers.

The poker table has always been stereotyped as a men's club, full of foul-mouthed, potbellied knuckleheads ragging on each other and chomping cheap cigars. My experience has been the opposite, but that might be my living in San Francisco, not a town known for its knuckleheads, like, say, Pittsburgh, Chicago, Milwaukee, and so on. (If you ever want to know whether a city is known for its knuckleheadedness, just check to see if the local politicians close city offices and public schools when one of their professional sports franchises makes it to its respective championship. If so, it is a knucklehead city.)

With a reputation for cosmopolitan food and wine, a thriving arts community, and liberal political makeup, San Francisco is not exactly considered a blue-collar town. But long before Haight-Ashbury was a hippie haven and Fisherman's Wharf was a tourist trap, the city by the bay was a workingman's town, and that element is still alive in our Lions Clubs, our dive bars, and our church basements. Many of the more boisterous constituents of that community were here tonight. And they were drinking, gambling, and swearing at the top of their lungs. (They had to smoke their stogies outside, however.)

To be fair, many of the guys were affable and intelligent, and it was not their fault they were drowned out by—or caught up in—a rowdy crowd bent on living it up on a Saturday night away from the wife and kiddies. I had just played in a particularly austere game the night before, so I may have been slightly overwhelmed by a poker crowd that fit the rough-and-tumble typecast.

A poster at the front door advertised that first place paid *One Thousand Dollars!!!* Second place paid half that, and third place paid $300. That was $1,800 total. Eighty players at $100 a head meant there was eight grand in the pool. This couldn't be right, and I went looking for J during the first break. The figures on the flyer were only what they could guarantee, not knowing how many players would show up, he told me. He gave me a sheet with revised payout figures. Eight places were paid, totaling $4,800.

I asked J what exactly the Men's Club was. They support the church by organizing events, doing maintenance, and raising money. Most of the members had kids in the parish school, so it was a good way to get the parents together. Over his shoulder, all I saw was a drunken throng of dads gambling away the school supply money, but I nodded appreciatively. J and another Men's Club officer put these tournaments together to raise money for the church. The last tournament, he told me, sucked in enough dough to install a new automatic garage door for the monsignor's carport.

And no wonder. The church took a 40 percent rake and got away with it. The World Series of Poker takes only 3 percent, and players bitch about that being too high. Here, most of the beer and food was donated, and the labor was all volunteer. Of course they had to buy all the chips, cards, and green felt, but it was still a tidy profit for unlocking the doors and turning on the lights. A few more tournaments and the monsignor could have something nice to park in his fancy new garage.

*Is there a women's club?* I asked.

*Yeah, but it's called the Mothers' Club.*

*Why don't they call the Men's Club the Fathers' Club?*

*I don't know. Probably so it doesn't look like a group of priests.*

*Ah. What does the Mothers' Club do?*

He motioned toward the food tables, where the women were serving meatball sandwiches, filling beer cups, and cleaning up.

*You're kidding me.*

*Hey, we clean the gutters and fix the benches,* he said.

*Still . . . Anyway, how are you able to host a poker tournament? Aren't there some legal issues?*

J was a lawyer, and a pretty smart one. He brushed off the question by mumbling something about the bingo license covering all the bases, as far as he knew. He looked at me suspiciously and ended that portion of our conversation. He led me over to a table being covered with felt. There were enough players out who were interested in playing a one-table tournament. We all shook hands and took seats.

I reminded myself to play my best game. Just because these guys were knocked out early did not mean all of them were saps. We all agreed to put fifty bucks in the kitty, and the winner and second place would get paid. J came along and tried to take two hundred for the house. I was the only one who balked, but J backed down and left with only a C-note.

While I shuffled the deck and the older fellas drank beer and hollered among themselves, a guy my age joined the table. He was wearing a 49ers jersey, like half the room, and an S.F. Giants hat, like the other half of the room. He immediately started telling his tragic tale of getting knocked out of the main event. If I have the story right, he went all-in with two pair while the board showed four diamonds. Someone had the ace and he was out. This didn't even qualify as a bad beat, but to him it was an injustice for the ages.

While I was very glad to have him at the table, I didn't want to actually talk to him. I could feel him staring at me, trying to place me from the neighborhood without success. His mouth was slightly agape, which, I soon learned, was basically its permanent position. His eyes were big and dull. I tried not to look at him, but I could tell that he had decided to talk to me and there was nothing I could do about it, so I glanced up and he gave me one of those "what's up" nods.

*Hey man, I'm Paul,* he said.

*Nice to meet ya, I'm Pat.*

*Pat? Hey, like the movie. You ever see that movie* It's Pat?

It's been at least fifteen years since Julia Sweeney played an androgynous character named Pat on *Saturday Night Live* and no one saw the spin-off movie, but occasionally someone will still bring her/him up when I introduce myself as Pat. The character was never that funny or that popular to begin with, but certain morons think referencing the "It's Pat" skit is a scream. And often they are Irish guys who should know better. It's not as much of a cross to bear as it would be if my mother had named me Gaylord, but it's a pain in the butt from time to time, like now, when I was talking to slack-jawed Paul. Regardless, I was very happy to have him at my table.

**Poker has many colorful** names for different player types, most of them based on living creatures, including lions, mice, fish, bulls, pigeons, turkeys, donkeys, and whales. Outside the animal kingdom, there are rocks, calling stations, leather asses, sheriffs, sliders, ribbon clerks, sandbaggers, suckers, shills, and maniacs. There is a special word in poker for a player who possesses annoying habits and insufferable attitudes that ruin the game on many levels. He not only takes the fun out of the game for you but scares away novice players who might be good for some action. He never shuts up and always has an insult or stupid comment ready to heave forth. In poker circles, this man is called an *asshole* (pronounced 'as-,[h]ōl).

Playing poker means suffering fools, and if you can't stand an asshole, perhaps you should take up a game without any. I recommend solitaire. Every game or sport has assholes, there are just more in poker.

If you get an asshole at your table, you shouldn't complain. Assholes are generally easier to beat than nice guys. Nice guys are even-tempered and have more perspective on losing and bad luck.

They are more likely to laugh off a bad beat and less likely to go on tilt. Assholes whine like babies every time things don't go their way. If you find yourself at a table full of nice, polite people, get up and leave. But I wouldn't worry about it too much because the odds of finding yourself at a table full of nothing but nice people are the same as flopping a royal flush.

There are two types of assholes you will deal with in poker. The first is the natural asshole and the other is the actor, someone deliberately performing the part of an asshole. A natural is someone who is just a jerk who cannot find others to sit with him at a table unless there is money on the table, and the actor is someone who has found a way to win without good cards.

I've had the privilege of playing with some great assholes. It has been an honor for me because I do well against them. One of the strongest aspects of my game is my ability to appreciate the theater without taking it personally. I developed this skill primarily from knowing numerous assholes and considering some of them friends. There are those who say that I, myself, am at least part asshole, but I try not to bring it to the poker table.

I knew Paul was a purebred natural asshole the second I met him. To sweeten the deal, he was also a moron. And drunk to boot! If I found out he was also rich, I was going to faint.

Be they natural or actor, assholes are not hard to identify, as they usually announce their presence before you sit down. It can, however, be difficult to tell one type from the other. One way is to look at their play. Naturals tend to win on lucky draws, whereas actors get people to call with lesser cards or fold the best hand. The way to beat a natural is to put pressure on him with a good hand rather than let him do it to you with a bad one.

The actor is tougher, but if he acts like he wants you to call, fold. If he acts like he wants you to fold, then raise. Most actors are rocks. They make a lot of noise to get people to play back at them, but they usually have it when they do. They want you to fantasize about breaking their bank so that you make a move on them when they have the nuts. This doesn't mean they don't bluff. If they think you have a marginal hand, they will bet at you and dare you to call. They are counting on your fear of losing to them and being humiliated as being a good reason for you to fold.

You must find ways to make both types work for you. Assholes make a game wild and unpleasant, and their annoying behavior makes people want to leave, so they play looser with their chips. When an asshole sets somebody on tilt, other players can potentially profit.

The trick is ignoring the behavior of the natural and never taking your eyes off what the actor is doing.

Waiting for the first deal, I sized up the table and my plan to beat it. I was going to play tight but solid poker. There was plenty of aggression at the table already, and I could sit back and wait for cards to double up. Only two other players had the look of grim determination marking a serious player. The rest were joshing around and pounding beers.

I would not bluff even once. You can't bluff drunken players, but you can pick them off when they try to bluff you. Drunks are at their most dangerous when loaded, and God, being a particularly cruel entity, saves his sweetest graces for idiots and sots—particularly on the river.

I also vowed that I would take advantage of position, if for no other reason than to give it a whirl. Honestly, I never put much stock in playing position. Every poker book preaches the importance of position, but I had never really seen the net effect. Ultimately, it's your cards against their cards. You either have the best hand or you don't. Where you sit can't matter that much. Being the last to act in a hand is great if no one has called and you want to try to steal the blinds, but can position play be that big a deal, pardon the pun?

Conventional poker wisdom holds that to play position well means waiting until you are the last or one of the last to act in a hand. The best position is the dealer, and the worst is immediately to his left, in the small blind. The dealer will always act last, and the small blind will always act first. The idea is that if you act later, you have more information via bets, calls, and raises ahead of you. If you get a sense that someone has a strong hand, you can fold. If the small blind makes a bet first, he may get raised many times over as the action goes around the table, and he has a tough decision when it is his turn again.

This already looked to be a wild game, and I didn't need any more tough choices. The earlier my position, the better my cards had to be. If I was under the gun, I better have aces or kings to call. If I was in the middle, I should have a decent-sized pair or ace/king suited to call. I would dump a lot of hands I used to play, like a pair of threes or queen/jack suited, because I was out of position. When I had the puck or was in the cutoff seat—just to the right of the dealer—I would be allowed to step on the gas a bit more and play weaker hands.

I folded the first fifteen hands in a row. When I had something interesting, like ten/nine suited, I was out of position, and when I had the button in front of me, I had crap cards. My tablemates were having a ball betting on everything. One guy had almost doubled his stack, and he had played every hand. Paul was in every hand too, but with his mouth and not his cards. He kept talking. He asked everyone if they had seen the game without specifying what sport. Whether or not they had seen the game did not alter his blabbering. When he had exhausted the table, he stopped other guys who were just walking by to ask them about the game or tell them his bad-beat story. He called everyone he had ever met "dawg." I achieved dawg status after saying I had missed seeing the game. *Damn, dawg, you missed a good game. How could you miss that game?* I told him, *I have it on TiVo, so don't tell me what happened.* That didn't work because he had to talk about it with the guy on my right and the guy on my left.

Paul liked the word *fag* a great deal. He called his buddy over by saying, *Hey, come here, fag!* He used it as a noun and a verb, in the same sentence. *You totally fagged out, you fag.* He even used the idiomatic *fagotized.*

Even with my vast experience dealing with his kind, my patience was wearing thin. Another player named Leo, thank God, had had enough and firmly but politely asked him to shut up and play. That worked for five minutes as he muttered to himself instead. When Paul started talking again as he bet, Leo made a big raise. I could tell Paul had nothing, and I was pretty sure Leo was raising out of frustration. I bet half my stack immediately. Paul folded. Leo looked pretty uncomfortable. This was the first pot I had entered, and I was upping the size of the pot. He sweated it out a moment or two and folded. I made a tidy sum and suddenly this position thing seemed dandy.

Another player, who wasn't even in the hand, asked me if I had even looked at my cards. Sure enough, my cards sat slightly askew right where they had been dealt.

*Of course,* I told him. *As soon as I got them. Usually, I wait until it's my turn, but I've been getting junk and I was due for a big hand.*

He seemed unsatisfied but didn't say any more. I made sure to alternate between looking at my cards in turn and looking at them when the deal was complete, just so my story stuck.

I was calm and collected but was doing triple axels in my head. I had taken down a big pot confidently without even looking at my cards; what a fucking stud I am. Poker God Doyle Brunson says he can take down the average table without even seeing his cards as long as the other players are unaware that he's playing blind. I used to think that was hyperbole, but I believe it now.

Leo was soon knocked out, never having recovered from his laydown. To my great pleasure, both the guys I had pegged as serious players went out too. Paul won a few pots by outdrawing better hands, and now he was having fun, which meant he was laughing. His laugh was a little bit donkey bray mixed with monkey screech, and he did not care if you didn't like it; in fact, he thought it was funny if you didn't like it, and you know what that means.

Assholes bother serious players more than hobbyists, and I could trace back both solid players' demise to the moment that Paul felt tickled. I kept telling myself that I was playing the table and not one guy, but I was rattled too. I really hated this guy.

An hour into the game, five of us were still alive, and I was contemplating dumping my chips and going to the bar. I still had half a beer in front of me, but that was just for show. It was the same beer I'd gotten when I came in. I wanted to play totally sober but didn't want to look like a shark by drinking water. We had all started with $200 in chips, and I had picked up a couple of good pots and was in second place with about $460 in chips. Beside me, Johnny was short-stacked with $190. Phil, who would have been a pretty good player if he had just a little more gamble in him, had $310. Mark sat to his left and had almost exactly the same as me with $450. It grated all of us that Paul was the chip leader with $590. Of course, he wouldn't shut up about it.

It seemed like such an ordinary hand when it started. We were playing $10/$20, having only raised the blinds once since the game began. Mark made the minimum raise from under the gun, and Paul called it. I looked at my cards and found a pair of sixes, which isn't bad when you're short-handed, so I called the $40. Johnny, who kept saying he had to get home or his girlfriend was going to kill him, called. Phil, the big blind, took his time, but he called.

The flop came down ten/nine/six, all clubs. I was elated to see my three of a kind but did not like the flush and straight possibilities at all. I would have a tough decision coming my way, but at least I was last to act. I knew Johnny was actually serious about leaving this time when he pushed all his chips into the center and put on his coat and screamed at the guy who was giving him a ride to wait a minute. Phil called the all-in and so did Mark. Paul had gotten up from the table to chase down someone who hadn't heard his bad-beat story. Mark shouted to him that there was a raise to him. Paul shouted back that he called and he'd be right back. We all shrugged and merrily tossed his chips into play.

I thought that at least my decision to fold was easy. In any normal game, when someone goes all-in and gets a caller, one of them has a good hand. When an all-in gets four callers, someone has a great hand. You better have the top possible straight flush to call or you are beat. I did not have a straight flush or even a straight. I had the low set of trips. Any two cards making a straight beat me, as did any other trips. Any two clubs had me beat. This is an easy laydown in any game. Or was it?

Johnny went all-in just to get out of the game and not have to pay for a cab. He certainly didn't seem happy to have three callers, like he would if he had a flush or a straight. He seemed to be waiting to get this over with. I do not give him credit for anything serious. Phil was a tight player who had gone all-in preflop twice before with a pair, which he kindly showed both times, and he always called with drawing hands. He would not have slow-played a pair, and I never saw him play low suited connectors like eight/seven, especially out of position. He most likely had ace/king and thought it was good against Johnny and guessed he'd be the only caller. Mark always talked about pot odds and had carefully counted the chips before calling. If he had a made hand, he would have raised. He didn't slow-play anything. I put him on a flush or straight draw or both and thought he felt like gambling. Paul wasn't even at the table and didn't even see the flop. He could have a pair, which would explain why he would call blind. Besides, he was dumb as a bag of hammers. I really thought I had the best hand, so I raised all-in.

The disgusted looks that hung on Phil's and Mark's mugs were two of the prettiest things I've ever seen. Phil only had a few chips and threw them in like they were made of feces. Mark was pot-committed too, and he called. Again, we shouted that there was a raise on the table to Paul, and he bellowed back impatiently, *I fucking call! Damn!* It was clear to me that he didn't know this was the same hand and almost all his chips were going into play.

Johnny had a queen of clubs and a ten of spades. Phil had an ace of spades and a king of clubs. Mark had the ace of clubs and a seven of hearts. Paul had a pair of jacks, including the club. The turn was a three of diamonds, and the river was a ten of diamonds, which gave me a momentary heart attack and Johnny a momentary orgasm. He almost shouted at his ride to leave him behind, but we saw suddenly that the ten that gave him trips gave me a full house and a monster stack of chips.

It took me three minutes to shake everyone's hand and stack my chips. I was just finishing up when Paul came back. Phil's and Mark's expressions were no longer the most beautiful thing I had ever seem. It took Paul about fifteen seconds to grasp what had happened, even though Phil was still there to explain it to him. I think he stuck around just to see this glorious, glorious moment.

After the change of dynamics sunk in a bit, Paul sat down behind his $130 of chips while I organized my $1,870 into colorful pilings. *This won't last too long,* I thought, though I was still nervous. *All you need is a chip and a chair* is an old poker truism for a reason. If he doubled up three times, he would be the chip leader. I wasn't going to take anything for granted. Besides, I could wait for cards and he could not.

I didn't have to wait long. I got dealt an ace/queen suited on the first deal, a nice hand heads-up. I went all-in and Paul sweated it out for a minute. *Fuck it, I call,* he said and turned over two kings, the second-best hand possible. Cowboys, as they're known, are good for a raise in a ten-handed game. In heads-up, they are a dream come true. If the deliberative act had been performed by anyone other than Paul, I might have considered it slow-rolling, the despicable act of having the best cards and waiting until your opponent thinks he has won before turning them over. Slow-rolling is the act of a *prick,* another obscure poker term. Even assholes hate slow-rollers. But Paul wasn't slow-rolling; he was legitimately considering a fold on the 1-in-110 chance that I had a pair of aces.

I shook my head in disgust while Paul got up from his chair and paced around. He must have seen that on television. A dozen players who had been knocked out of the main tournament were crowded around us, waiting for the game to be over so they could play another losers' game. Phil had stayed at the table to deal for us and keep his seat for the next game. He dealt the flop and I caught an ace right out of the gate. It took Paul a minute to get it, but when the turn and river were blanks, it sunk in and he started telling his bad-beat story to the guy standing next to him, even though that person had just seen the whole thing.

Paul got $100 for his second-place finish, which he lost in five minutes during the next game. I played another losers' table and came in second place for a hundred bucks. I didn't get involved in any overly dramatic hands, and I didn't push to top my first win. When I bet, I had strength or sensed weakness. When I folded, I did so to better hands. I grinded out a few chips here and there and built my stack up by earning pots. Chiefly, I avoided trouble by making sure that I played position as best I could.

With my first and second finishes, I was up $375, after I kicked in $25 for the reverend's new Caddy. The losers' table allowed a much greater profit percentage than the actual tournament, and they were still playing, whereas I was leaving with some stone-cold cash.

I won by playing smart and learning from my mistakes. I had been patient and played good cards. I bet aggressively and made good reads on the other players. Mostly, I had used position to my advantage, and that was a factor in every single pot I won. In the big pot, I would have folded from any seat other than the button. Being last allowed me to see what the other players were doing and why. Going all-in turned out to be the right move, but if I had decided to fold, it wouldn't have been too bad either. I'd still be second in chips, and Paul would still be almost broke. If I had been in Mark's seat with a pair of sixes, I would have folded to the all-in call. But being the last to act gave me a view of the big picture and the opportunity to make a strong play. I was way off in my initial attitude toward position, and it is damn easy to admit you're wrong about something with a pile of cash in your pocket. All this shit was starting to make sense and, more important, was becoming profitable. I felt so good pulling out of the parking lot that I gave Paul, who was sitting at the bus stop, a friendly honk as I drove home a winner.

**Gus's had a horseshoe bar,** a small restaurant area, and a banquet room in the back. From the looks of it, the last banquet held there was a celebration of Harry Truman's reelection. It was filled with broken chairs that no one would ever get around to fixing and boxes of Christmas decorations that were half empty because most of them stayed up year-round. The crowd ran the gamut from old folks on Social Security to kids testing out their new fake IDs. The walls were covered with objects that were once only ephemera and knickknacks but achieved permanence and significance after being there for a few years. It had the character that TGI Friday's and Bennigan's pay consultants a fortune to reproduce in facsimile. The bar top was scarred but spotless, the stools were permanently concaved from a thousand asses, and the brass rail was worn from being leaned upon by generations of tipplers. To me, the place is Shangri-la.

I had once heard from a very reliable source—the barfly next to me—that Gus hosted a poker game on Saturday before the bar opened and that occasionally he would let a new player sit in. Gus was one of the nicest guys I'd ever met, but he was nobody's fool.

Just because he smiled at you and laughed at your jokes did not mean he liked you. Just because he bought you a drink did not mean he considered you trustworthy. Hosting a poker game may be a minor infraction of the law if you do it in your kitchen, but it is a much more serious legal issue when you are playing on premises underneath the framed liquor license.

I wanted to wrangle an invitation, so I decided to stop by after work on a Friday. I figured I would have a few drinks to grease the skids, tip particularly well, and then drop some subtle hints about my interest in poker. The first part went fine, but Gus was nowhere to be found. The bartender said he was coming in soon, so I sat and waited. I waited a couple of hours and, before I knew it, my few drinks had a few drinks. When Gus walked in, I was in my cups and, if memory serves, had forgotten why I had come to the bar in the first place. It turned out that Gus had only stopped in briefly to pick something up, and as he walked back out the door, I recovered my memory and chased him, catching him as he was getting into his car. *Hey, Gus, can I come to your poker game tomorrow?* I slurred out. He glanced at my drunken ass and said, *Sure. Noon. Here.*

The next morning, my hangover and I showed up half an hour late and knocked on the door. I knocked on the door again and waited. It was only twelve thirty, but it was shaping up to be a tough day. I had walked in the door three hours late the night before, and my good news—getting a seat in a poker game, at a bar, the next afternoon—failed to impress my darling bride. She reminded me that I had promised to take our son to the zoo. This was bad. I can justify a lot of things for the sake of selfish convenience, but I couldn't blow off my son to play cards with a bunch of rummies at a saloon. But I didn't know if Gus would save a seat for me or hold the game up until I arrived. I didn't want to burn my bridges with him if I didn't show up. I promised that I would play in the game at noon and be home by four o'clock to take my son to the zoo for a few hours.

I learned that day that the train schedules are very different on the weekends, and a good portion of my precious poker time was spent waiting anxiously on a platform. By the time I got to the bar, I was winded and sweaty from running ten blocks. Nobody came to the door after three knocks, and the place was locked tight as a drum. *Was the game canceled? Was this some sick joke? Was Gus teaching me a lesson?* Gus interrupted my paranoid delusions by opening the door. They were in the banquet room and hadn't heard me.

I find bars at midday very seductive. I hate big, happening scenes, and have since I was a young, single guy. The thought of bellying up to a packed bar to wait fifteen minutes for a beer is abhorrent to me. The only reason people like a full bar is because tight quarters can provide excuses for interacting with others. They need the coverage provided by a throng to pretend to act natural. I like going into a near-empty bar on a Tuesday afternoon, when you can find a seat without any problem and actually hear the person next to you. I like a place where you know your bartender and what songs are on the jukebox, a place like Gus's.

Gus led me to the back room. The junk had been pushed aside and some tables brought in from the restaurant. It was nothing fancy, but it was thrilling. In the old days, games like this went on all the time, but in these detestable modern days, very few survive. I think that is a shame.

In the working-class section of the city where I grew up, there was a bar called the Stein that I would walk past on my way to school. The front of the building was bricked up to prevent sunlight from coming in because it bothered the people drinking at 7:30 a.m. They went so far as to add a thick curtain around the inside of the front door so that anyone coming in wouldn't bring the dreaded light with them. In the back of the building, there was one small opaque window with a crack in it. If you peeked in it just so, as I did many times, you would see palookas drinking dollar boilermakers and playing poker at any time of the day or night. You won't see that now, however. My old neighborhood is the height of fashionable living. Old Heidi's Russian Bakery is now a boutique, the Fix-It shop is a sushi bar, and the Stein is a Jamba Juice, serving high-priced smoothies instead of cheap beers, and the only shots they sell are of blended wheatgrass.

I don't know who I expected would be at the game at Gus's, but I was surprised to see a table full of very old people. I'm old enough to remember life before MTV and cell phones, but every one of these guys had seen Halley's comet with their own eyes at least twice. One was in a wheelchair, and another had an oxygen tank that he rolled behind him. I figured I couldn't smoke around the flammable tank until one of the guys lit a More cigarette. The other men called Gus "kid," and he was at least sixty-five. Gus introduced me around, and I said *Hello,* loudly. Remembering everybody's name was easy. They all looked exactly like what they had been christened. Fred looked just like Fred Mertz from *I Love Lucy.* Mickey had big ears that hung perpendicular to his skull. Tip had bloodshot eyes and a bulbous nose. Barney just looked like a Barney.

A hand had just ended, so I took the empty seat next to Gus and handed him my $100 and took my chips. The cards were pushed to me to deal. I had shuffled up and started spreading the cards when Fred asked, *What game we playing?* I froze. What the hell could that mean? Gus broke in and said they played dealer's choice here, but it was limited to three games. Five-Card Draw, Seven-Card Stud, and Baseball were the only choices. *What the hell is Baseball?* I thought. *Baseball is Seven-Card Stud with threes and nines wild,* Mickey said without me asking. *We play a good bit of Baseball here. It's fun, you'll see.*

Right. I couldn't wait. He'd probably want to play 52-card pickup next. I actually thought about excusing myself and leaving. Was I really going to sit down and play games I didn't know with guys old enough to have invented them? But I was already there, and perhaps this could lend some variance to my

Hold 'em game. Did he say threes *and* nines were wild or threes *through* nines? No matter, I was going to fold at the first opportunity every time that game was dealt.

Five-Card Draw and Seven-Card Stud were games I've known since I was a kid, but being familiar with the rules was one thing and playing good enough to win money was an entirely different block of cheese.

*No Texas Hold 'em?* I asked, hopefully. *No Texas Hold 'em,* the unanimous chorus replied. Obviously, I was not the first to suggest adding the game. I hadn't played draw poker in ten years, and, for all I knew, Baseball was dealt faceup. I called Seven-Card Stud and continued to deal. I knew a little about the game, but not much. If you have good cards, raise. If you have a very good draw, call. If you have neither, fold. Like I said, not much.

In the game, everyone antes $1 and the high card starts the action. In many Seven-Card Stud games there's a forced bet, usually four times the ante, by the highest or lowest card, but Gus and company didn't play that way. The minimum bet was $2, and the maximum raise was $4 until fifth street, when it doubled.

I had the ace showing and was delighted to find another in the hole alongside a trey. I bet $2 hoping someone would call. Everyone called. Okay. I dealt another card to everyone, and nobody paired up or matched their suits, and it was too early to worry much about straights. I got a queen to keep my aces company. I liked my hand, but I would've been happy to take the pot right away, so I bet $4. Everyone called again. No griping or moaning, just flat calls. They didn't even seem to be thinking about it. I dealt another round and everyone got something that scared me, but I landed another ace. It was still up to me to act. I thought about checking, but you can't slow-play aces when everyone can see most of them. Checking would basically announce that I had a spare bullet in my hand. I bet the full eight bucks, again hoping to get at least one caller. I got five.

It suddenly occurred to me that since they played this crazy Baseball game, maybe they had some wacky rules for Seven-Card Stud. From what I could see, my two aces were best and someone should fold. I dealt another round and paid close attention to what came up and how people reacted to their cards.

Gus now had 7♠/4♣/6♦/4♦. Fred had 3♠/5♥/3♥/9♣. Mickey had K♣/Q♥/5♣/5♦. Tip had 7♣/10♠/7♦/K♦. Barney had 2♠/4♥/7♥/K♠. I had A♠/Q♣/A♦/10♣.

What could everyone have? Who was happy right now and who was disappointed? Who got lucky and who got screwed? I couldn't get any reaction from their faces because they were so weather-beaten, no emotion could get through. I tried to make a quick assessment before I had to bet. Gus could have a straight, but he would need a five, and there were three of them out on the board already, so that wasn't likely. He could have three of a kind, but he probably would have raised before now. Fred couldn't have quads because I had his case three. He might have a full house. Mickey's fives were cheap, and he couldn't have a made straight or flush. Tip's sevens were all played out, and I had one of his tens. Barney's hand was just trash.

As far as I could tell, it was unlikely that anyone had me beat, and I had an ace-high flush draw just in case, but I would've still liked to have far fewer players to contend with. The table was getting a little impatient, so I bet the max again. Everyone called.

What the hell was going on with these crazy old coots?

I dealt the last card, saying the perfunctory comment, *down and dirty,* as I did. My last card was a five of spades, making Gus's and Barney's straights impossible and Fred's and Mickey's possible full houses less likely. I made the big bet out of what was, by now, sheer habit. Gus called, Fred called, Mickey called, Tip called.

Barney raised.

I was having the least fun I'd ever had at a poker table, and I was still playing the first hand. Even being as careful as I could be, I very well might have been missing something. Barney couldn't have a straight, and a full house was a long shot. I wasn't worried about three of a kind. He had two hearts showing. Could he have three hearts in the hole? He must because there was no other possible hand that he could raise with. Why had he called all those bets earlier with a long-shot draw?

I was baffled. Thirty-one dollars in the pot with eight more to call. It would cost me almost half my chips if I lost. I looked at my cards again and tried to go over the hand one more time, but I heard several irritated sighs around the table. For $8 more I had a slim chance of winning almost $200. I decided the pot odds were too good to pass up and I said, *Call.* Like an echo, I heard, *Call, Call, Call, Call* from the others. I hated that damn word.

Gus turned up his cards first. He had two pair and a busted straight draw. Fred had three treys. Mickey had an ace and a pair of jacks in the hole to go with his fives. Tip held a pair of twos and a ten to make sevens and tens. He tried to make a case that three pair should count for something, but he was rebuffed. I didn't even care what anyone else had. I wanted to see Barney's cards. He really should have shown them first, but protocol seemed a trifle lax here. He picked up his hand and looked at it one more time before throwing it away.

*Argh. I was just bluffing at it,* he growled.

I was chagrined to realize I still had my cards facedown, so I grabbed them and flipped up. After a moment of resigned, I-knew-it-type nods, I scooped in the pot. Gus grabbed the empty glasses and went up to the bar to refill them, and the others went for a bathroom break, which looked like it would take a good while. I looked at everyone's fully exposed hands and tried to figure out what had just happened. Were these guys the worst poker players on earth or was I that good? Or both?

Seeing everything now, I saw that it was neither. Everyone had a draw to a big hand, but they didn't bother to look around them to see how many of their outs—cards that could improve their hands—were already dead. Gus was drawing the last five and only made a meager two pair on the last card. Fred's chances of making a full boat with his threes were diminished by having his jack and five shared by other hands. Mickey had an ace in the hole so he probably figured I didn't. When he paired his jacks on the river, he figured they were good. Tip had a wired pair to start, which is strong, but he didn't dump them when they failed to improve, and getting a pair of sevens on his porch kept him in the hand. I quietly picked up Barney's hand and took a gander. Queen, six, nine, with only one heart. He had no straight draw, no flush draw, and no pair.

They all had a potential hand, except for Barney, but nothing unbeatable. They all made the mistake of chasing their draws by calling bets to see one more card. Hoping to catch a big hand is fine in any stud game, including Hold 'em, but if the hand you want has a high likelihood of being second best, you have to fold. Instead, they got in trouble when they caught second pairs and more draws. Even if their hands filled them up, no one was assured of winning because someone could easily have made a flush, a straight, or a full house. I had announced my strength at every opportunity by betting, which they all ignored. I wondered if they were just a little too lazy to read the table and see that the cards they needed were in someone else's hand, or if they were just so optimistic that they figured luck would carry the day. I pulled my notebook from my pocket and furtively scratched down everyone's hand so I could look at them later. Maybe I'd take up Seven-Card Stud and forget Hold 'em.

Gus came back and saw that I had flipped up Barney's cards and laughed, *That crazy bastard.*

He was crazy, but I had nearly dumped the best hand to him. If I had done that, I would have gone into the men's room and jammed my head into the urinal. Folding would have been a huge technical mistake, pot odds aside. With five other players in a hand who were married to their cards, there was a very good chance that I would be beat by at least one of them. *Bluff* magazine, one of the leading poker magazines, has a quiz every month so you can test your poker knowledge. If I had read the question:

*In a Seven-Card Stud game, your split trip aces have four callers to your bet and a raise behind you during the last hand. Do you:*

a. *Call*
b. *Raise*
c. *Fold*
d. *Fold and smack yourself in the head for getting into this much trouble.*

I would have confidently picked *d*. Instead, by reading the hand and capitalizing on the other players' missteps, I was stacking a big pile of chips. I read the board correctly, but, more important, I saw the other players weren't paying much attention to what everyone else had showing. This told me that their play would be handicapped by their having less information than I did. If, however, I noticed Mickey studying everyone's up cards and then calling, I would have figured he had a big hand because he'd be playing even though his two fives could not improve. If he had raised me and then been raised by Barney, I probably would have folded.

Everyone makes mistakes. Long ago, I worked in politics as a campaign manager. After a particularly bad day in which I had screwed up an endorsement and felt like the devil's idiot sister, the person who had hired me sat me down and told me not to worry. *The one who wins is not the person who is perfect,* he said. *The winner is the guy who made the least amount of mistakes.* Politics and poker are similar in that way (and in other ways too, including lying, conniving, being phony, and so on).

It took almost twenty minutes for everyone to sit back down and for Barney to bump into every piece of furniture on the way back. During the shuffle, I asked how long this game had been going on. The guesstimate was between fifteen and eighteen years. Barney was the only original player left, and Mickey was the new guy, having joined just six years before. I wondered if there had ever been any trouble with the cops. They chortled, and Fred told me they were all retired sheriff's deputies, except him. He used to be a parole officer. Tip warned me that I had better not be a basement dealer. Before I could protest, Gus assured them I was not.

**Since the next hand** was Baseball, I laid down my hand but tried to get a sense of the game. Everyone who stayed in until the end had a full house or better. Four tens won. Mickey dealt Baseball again, and again I threw my cards away. I had a big stack and could afford to play behind a log, as they say. Then Tip spread Seven-Card Stud. Barney had a king showing and led out with a $4 bet. I noticed his hand was shaking and remembered that in *Caro's Book of Poker Tells* it states that a bettor who is trembling has a big hand. The quivering isn't nervousness, as one would suspect, but the body inadvertently releasing tension. I had a lousy hand anyway and folded. Barney made what I thought was a nasty comment about my tight play, but he started coughing and I didn't hear exactly what he said. A guy his age having a coughing fit concerned me, and I wasn't the only one. All the players were silently watching him. He recovered and finished nicely with a ten-high straight he made on the last card.

When the deal was passed to Barney, everyone else put down their coffee cups and sat up in their chairs a bit. I did the same, not knowing why. While his left hand held the deck fairly steady, his right hand quaked violently. I had folded to what I thought was an obvious tell but was actually some sort of palsy. When he tried to skim the cards to the players, his fingers would invariably jerk and snap, and the cards would go flying into the air. I was right next to him so he simply placed my cards in front of me, but Gus had to stand up and clap his hands over the card and clutch it to his chest so no one could see it. Fred missed his card and it landed faceup on the floor. I turned away so I wouldn't be tempted to catch a glance. When the deal was over, Gus leaned into me and whispered, *We call that catching butterflies.*

Barney favored Five-Card Draw, jacks or better to open, and I only had a meager pair of threes. Gus opened for the minimum bet, and everyone called. I decided to call because, if I laid down early again, I think it would have induced a fatal cardiac episode for Barney.

After everyone drew cards and my hand didn't improve, I check-folded to Gus's bet and Mickey's raise. I did not care if this killed Barney, I was not betting out with a pair of treys.

When the dust settled, Fred had a straight flush to the king of hearts. This doesn't happen very often, and everyone was very excited. There is no shame in losing to the best hand in poker, so everyone was in a good mood. Fred told a long story about getting two straight flushes in a row back in 1972, so Gus had to tell his story about losing with four kings against a suited wheel.

As much as I enjoyed the jawboning, the deal had gone around only once in almost two hours. Every hand had been played to the last card, and nobody was in a hurry. I had to leave in the next hour and really wanted to get into a few more pots, so I dealt quickly and, as dealer, pushed the others to act quickly.

I wasn't seeing many good cards, and waiting while the others played was losing its considerable power to charm me. When any small thing reminded someone of something, the game stopped while someone told a story about it. I was the only one who seemed to mind, and I was beginning to mind very much. If I sat on my cards, I would be leaving a winner, but I felt like I could break the game if they would just stop strolling down memory lane and deal the damn cards.

I finally got a chance during a hand of Baseball. I had two threes in the hole and an eight of clubs showing to start and flat called a reraise so I wouldn't alert anyone. When my hand improved with a nine, I was beginning to believe Mickey's assertion that this was a fun game. By the last card, only Fred and I were still in the hand. He was showing a nine and two suited connectors and an ace, and I still had four of a kind. I called his bet and caught another eight down. Fred looked at his final card and bet the maximum.

I raised and Fred raised. He might have had me beat, so I called. He pulled two of his hole cards out and built a straight flush to the jack. I tossed my five of a kind and tried to grab the pot.

I don't know if I was more shocked by the strength of Fred's grip on my wrist or by the speed at which he lunged out of his seat to grab me. Clearly, Fred believed his straight flush to be good against five of a kind. As I put my palms up to show they held no chips and tried to wiggle out of his viselike grasp, Mickey started chiming, *Easy, easy, easy now.* Barney broke in with his gravelly voice, *Split the pot. Split pot.* Tip just placed his hand tightly over the rim of his glass so the melee wouldn't spill his whiskey sour. Gus simply got up and walked away without comment. He was as close as I had to a friend in this joint and he was gone.

It took a very long minute, but Fred calmed a bit and released me. I sat back down. Mickey seemed pleased that we took his advice. Tip licked the flat of his palm and picked his drink back up. Barney continued saying, *Split pot. Split the pot.*

Gus strolled back in with a tattered paperback book. He flipped through a few pages until he found what he was looking for. He announced that five of a kind beats a straight flush and that was that. Fred demanded to see the book. Unsatisfied, he tried to make the case that Baseball was different, but his three pair argument was still fresh in everyone's mind and he was denied. He then tried to glom on to Barney's split-pot theory, but when Fred turned to him for support, Barney didn't seem to know what he was talking about. Fred's apology seemed counterfeit, but I accepted it unconditionally, and when he explained his reasons for getting so upset, I unctuously concurred that he had every reason to be upset. I said I should have waited until the pot was conceded before taking the chips, so, actually, the whole mess was my fault. Fred didn't disagree and seemed satisfied enough to resume play.

As I watched the men trying to catch the butterflies, I realized I was already late. It was half past three, and my chances of finishing this hand and getting home by four were slim. I announced, albeit quietly, that this was my last hand. Fred took this to mean that I was still upset from the misunderstanding, as he called it, and he again went into his spiel about being justified in freezing the hand. I assured him as best I could that the last hand was ancient history. Mickey was just upset that I was leaving a winner, and the house rules said you had to give at least a one-round notice before leaving. I had been here three hours and we were just finishing our third round. Nobody seemed impressed by my story about taking my son to the zoo, which sounded fake, even to me. I looked to Gus, who must have felt some pity because he said I could go anytime I liked.

I was up $360-plus and resolved to dump some money back into the game. This is something card cheats do to throw suspicion off them, but I just wanted to get out without having a geriatric mob chasing me down the street. And I wanted to come back. I figured I'd raise and then fold after the draw. Fred opened and Mickey raised and Barney called and I raised and everyone called. There was a healthy pot, and I was glad to contribute. I dumped a pair of sixes and an ace and kept a jack and a ten. I paired my jack and my ten. I could still fold to any bet and defend it. I checked. So did everyone else. Gus had a busted straight. Fred's queens got no help. Mickey had a four flush. Barney had ace high.

I said I was sorry as many times as I could in the time it took to cash out. I offered to buy a round of drinks, but they were free. I promised to come back the next week, and I meant it. I would skip my sister's wedding to do it. *Yeah, yeah, yeah, take the money and run,* they all said. Gus walked me to the door to lock up after me. He told me the game broke up at four anyway, which was minutes away, and I was welcome back anytime.

I flagged a cab and sped home. With no weekday traffic, I would only be a few minutes late. Counting my $440 profit, it would be an extravagant trip to the zoological gardens today. I did feel a little guilty about taking so much money from some guys who are too old to buy green bananas, but with every mile closer to home my remorse dimmed. I played well and they played badly. I got lucky and they didn't. If I had lost, not even one of the old goats would have felt a tinge of remorse. I had lost plenty in the past, and, with a few exceptions, I didn't blame the guy who outplayed me. I played my best poker, except the last hand, and I earned my money. I should not have even tried to dump the last hand, although it is ironic that if I had drawn to my pair of sixes, I would have lost.

Playing my best game all the time was what I'd been working for. I hoped the guys wanted me back again, but if they didn't, I'd find another game. Maybe the zookeepers had a poker night.

**With my newfound** wealth and my gigantic poker testicles I decided it was time to hit the real tables. I had been avoiding card clubs and casinos, preferring to cut my teeth on old men, youngsters, and dear friends. But it was time. If I was going to have any chance of winning the World Series of Poker, I had to get serious and win at competitive levels.

My game was red-hot, and, when I sat at a table, I expected to win. Over a couple of months, I had found and sat in on a variety of games and done well at some and done really well at others. I did lose a few times, but that was to be expected, and I was never really unhappy with my play. You can play well and still lose, sometimes. Over time, good play produces wins and therefore a profit.

I had steadily moved up in my online career and was winning consistently playing $20 sit-and-go tournaments. Sit-and-goes are one-table contests where you start with six or ten players and play until there is only one left, although the top two or three get paid.

Getting more experience was paying off too. Situations that seemed foreign just months ago now seemed rote. If someone raised me, I generally knew what it meant. More and more of the game seemed comfortable and familiar. But staying in a cozy place wasn't an option.

My very first visit to a card club was just a walk-through years ago, and it was dark, seedy, and unfriendly. I wasn't looking forward to stepping into another one. I drove a few miles to the township of Colma, a community famous for its many cemeteries and for having more dead residents than live ones. But Colma is more that just a giant boneyard; it also has malls. Lucky Chances Casino sits right between the Serramonte Mall and the Italian Cemetery. To my delight, it was none of the things I remembered a card room being.

The decor was a little cheesy, with floor-to-ceiling mirrors and brass-plated fixtures and a carpet pattern that induced headaches if you stared at it too long. But it didn't smell like a bus station men's room, and there was some actual sunlight allowed in. The staff was friendly despite having to wear goofy uniforms. The women had white Western blouses with string ties, and the men had collarless shirts and glittery vests. Most fortunately, none of the customers gave me the Look. The Look is a glance that says, *Are you a cop? You better not be a cop. I hate cops.*

I walked through the joint like I owned it. I did not want anyone to know I was a card-room virgin. I watched some people come in and walk over to a desk to sign in, then head to a table. I watched some of the games from the rail, picked up some flyers for upcoming tournaments, and was soon itching to get started. The woman at the desk asked me what game I wanted to play. *Hold 'em,* I said. She pointed behind her to a large whiteboard with twenty columns. Above every row were the names, stakes, and buy-ins for the games. There were various levels of Omaha, Razz, Stud, and Lowball. For Hold 'em there were five levels of limit, from $2/$4 to $40/$80, and no-limit starting at $1/$1/$3 and going up. I pointed to the lowest no-limit table, and she wrote my name down beneath a bunch of others. *The floorman is opening a new table so it shouldn't take too long,* she said. *I'll let him know it's your first time.*

The floorman was car-salesman nice, and he gave me a quick rundown of the rules as he walked me over to table 31. *In one/ one/three, the dealer posts a one-dollar bet, the small blind puts up a buck, and the big is three. You'll have to post a big blind when you sit down. It is then four dollars to call. When you sit down, put your money on the table and the dealer will call for a chip runner. The minimum buy-in is fifty dollars, and the maximum is a hundred. Every half hour we change dealers and collect the rake. The rake is six dollars every half hour. No taking chips off the table during play. It's called rat-holing, and it is not allowed. No string bets. Tip your dealers. Good luck.* He said all this in ten seconds, and I got the sense he said it fifty times a day.

I was seated in a sliver of space between a very large woman and a very large Asian man. The table didn't look too sinister, but there was one man there who looked suspiciously like Johnny Chan, the two-time world champion of poker. What would Johnny Chan be doing at a $3 table? *I need to settle down,* I told myself. I got my chips, peeked at my cards, and bet.

A couple of hours later, I went outside to take a cigarette break. The dealer button was across the table, and if I didn't take too long, I'd be back at the table in time for the puck. The dealer would subtract my blinds, but it was worth it. If I missed a pair of aces, tough. I sat on a bench and thought about what was happening at the table. I was not playing my best poker. I had not used an ounce of guile. When I bet, I had barely thrown sissy slaps instead of haymakers. My table image was that of a wallflower. I had pulled no slick moves. On the drive over, I had scripted some intricate trap plays and defensive counterattacks to overly aggressive bullies who wanted to steal my blinds. By the time I got to the table, these seemed like scenes out of some old movie I had once seen, not viable options.

But I was winning. I was up at least $50.

For some people, knowledge builds up in their brains slowly, like plaque. For others, it is a kick in the teeth. I'm of the latter variety. What occurred to me was that these guys were not that good. They didn't play amazing, cutthroat poker. One guy actually used his fingers to count the number of outs he had. With a few exceptions, they were tight/passive players. People who called a lot and folded to raises, provided the raise was big enough.

The image I'd had of my would-be opponents was of pockmarked ex-cons, pimp operators, and steely-eyed grifters, but I found myself surrounded by jovial retirees and twenty-something pretenders who wore sunglasses. There were a couple of possibly solid players who played selective hands in good position, but they folded a lot when confronted with a big raise. I reckoned they had recently switched from limit to no-limit. I didn't play many hands, and when I did, I bet the size of the pot. The one time I was reraised, I went all-in and the guy folded. I had not had to show my cards yet, not that I would have been ashamed to. I had decent made hands or strong draws.

Mostly, I played when I was out. I paid attention to who bluffed a lot and who tried to call their way to victory. I cocked my head a notch so I was staring directly at the player during their turn. I wanted them to know I was watching everything. I tried to guess what hand they were holding, and every now and again I was right. I tried to make my table image active. When a player folded to a big bet, I would try to catch his eye and nod so he would think that I would have done the same thing. I like this little trick because if you want someone to believe you are smart, tell them you agree with them.

Two people at the table concerned me. The first was Lipstick Lady, who used her time out of play to apply and reapply dusty rose color to her mouth. She had a large stack of chips and used them to muscle people around. The other was GORE-TEX man. He looked like a forty-something who had recently bought a mountain bike to strap on top of his Subaru Outback. He was the most aggressive player at the table and one of the few to talk a lot.

I hadn't tangled with either yet. The three of us were content to carve the others up. I played fewer hands but won every one. GORE-TEX was two seats to my left, but I had not attempted to steal his blinds because every time I had the dealer position, I had junk hands. But it was only a matter of time.

I had a real hand on the button, a pair of queens, and I made a pot-sized bet. GORE-TEX was not happy to see his blind go into my stack, and he raised me. I had seen him do this before. If someone appeared to be trying to steal his big blind, he raised back at them. This is fine, as poker practices go, but you have to be careful because someone might have a strong hand, like I did then.

I reraised him by grabbing a stack of chips in each hand and shoved them forth. Queens are a great hand, but they are vulnerable, and I'd be happy to take the pot now. A call wouldn't have killed me either. I was happy with either option.

Instead, GORE-TEX man announced that I had made a string bet, a form of cheating.

A string bet occurs when a player makes a partial bet and, watching for a reaction from the other player, will complete the bet or go back into his stack for more chips and raise.

In my case, I put a stack of chips in each hand and put both my hands in at the same time and said, *Raise*. He called it to the dealer, who told me to take my raise back. A young player at the table protested that it was not a string bet. The floorman was called over and asked the dealer if I actually went back into my hand for more chips. The dealer said yes. He lied. GORE-TEX man sat smugly. The kid across the table shook his head in disgust. I took my bet back. I knew for a fact now that GORE-TEX was on a draw. When I saw the flop, it had very little help for someone looking for a straight or a flush. He checked, I made a large bet, and he folded to me.

Even losing the hand, GORE-TEX looked self-satisfied. He got to see the flop, even if it didn't help him. I knew he didn't care about the pot; he thought he had put me on tilt and would soon be profiting from it. He guessed I would start playing revenge poker and come after him with less than premium hands. I kept calm and played my cards. I didn't chase him into any pots or avoid him. My doing nothing, oddly enough, made him nervous, and after the dealer was cycled to another table, he requested a table change. I stayed for the duration and cashed out $170 up. Not the biggest payday, but no small feat for my first day. I even saved a little money by refusing to tip that particular dealer.

**I returned to Lucky Chances** several times in the following weeks and had only one losing session. My one loss was due to pride, and I beat myself up over it pretty good. Now, if I have a prideful thought, I put a lit cigarette out on my eyelid. That should teach me.

After feeling pretty good about my game, I decided it was time to enter a tournament. Lucky Chances hosts one six days a week, so one Saturday I put on my best poker face and headed to the city of the dead loaded for bear.

The tournament began at ten thirty in the morning. I had called the night before to put my name on the sign-up sheet, which I was assured was unnecessary. I arrived half an hour early and went to the cashier to pay my entry fee. She directed me to another window that was devoted exclusively to tournaments. I quietly wandered over, making sure no one noticed that I had gone to the wrong window and could tag me as a naïf. Nobody could give a rat's ass. Nobody was hanging back in the shadows trying to get reads on the crowd, and if they were, they would give me nary a thought.

A lot of people seemed out of place and stood around reading free copies of *Poker News* or watching ESPN. The only places to stand were in front of the cage near the exit, a high-traffic area. Every few seconds a busboy carrying a tray, a dealer pushing a chip cart, or a great big fat person heading to the bathroom would force you to move. The only inlet where you could wait unmolested was at the bottom of the ramp leading to the playing area, but that spot was for regulars only, and it was full.

I had been to the casino on different days of the week and at various hours of the day, and I was always surprised to see many of the same faces. Some of those people lived there. Fifteen men and a few women stood in what was clearly their space, waiting for their seats to open. They chatted up the staff walking by and teased each other about some past occurrence. Where we newbies were mute, they were loud. On the bulletin board near the cashier was a group of pictures of recent tournament winners, and they were all regulars. What surprised me more was the diversity of the card-room clique.

They ranged in age from the early twenties to those born in the early twenties. They were Asian, white, Hispanic, and black. Some had bright pearly whites, and some had only the one tooth. It occurred to me that poker could do what fifty years of tolerance education, social programs, and Benetton ads could not: unite everyone under a common flag, a cash-green flag with a big poker chip in the middle. I was getting *verklempt*, so I left the in-crowd to themselves and went to the shop to buy myself a V8.

I like V8. At home, I buy it by the case or the gallon jug and drink it with abandon. Nearly all serious poker players avoid drinking alcohol while at the tables. Most drink bottled water or coffee. V8 is rarely available in restaurants, but at Lucky Chances, and at many casinos and card clubs I've been to since, the bar and gift shop always stock plenty of it. Many players who are sitting for many hours will drink the scarlet brew rather than have a meal. I am now wary when an opponent is downing V8. I left a table once when I saw someone mixing the juice with Red Bull.

You can't stand in the playing area, but you can walk through it. I used the opportunity on the way back from the gift shop to look for my table. My card said table eight, seat one. I found tables seven and nine but no table eight. When they announced that the tournament seating would begin, I had to ask someone for directions. Table eight was between tables two and six.

While the tables were random, the seats were not, and seat one is always to the dealer's left. I sat down and waited. The first-timers and the infirm were the only ones who sat at the first call. The regulars stayed jawing among themselves until the tournament director came and harangued them to take their places. They fell into place just as the dealer dealt for the button.

I was under the gun and looked down at a king/ten of hearts. I threw my cards into the muck, resolved to my strategy of only playing speculative hands in good position. Two players called and the flop came out king/king/ten.

Players not in the hand are not supposed to react to the flop. It gives an active player hand information that he didn't earn by betting. So I sat stoically until the hand was over, when I wasn't able to resist telling the player next to me that I would have flopped a full house, kings full of tens. *Yeah, sure,* he said, *me too.*

Picking your spots to get aggressive in poker is more art than science, and much more so in a poker tournament. Three players went all-in in the first round. In a cash game, this happens every couple of hours. There's a philosophy that you should double up early or go bust. For the regulars at my table, this was very much part of their philosophy. The cash games were their bread and butter, and time away from those tables cost them money. If they were going to play a tournament, they were going to take the lead and keep it or go bust. There's always another one tomorrow, they thought.

I hoped I could catch a nice high pair and sucker one of these maniacs to put all their chips into a pot against me. I wasn't the only one to have this idea. Forty-five minutes into the tournament, a gray-haired man in a red shirt across from me, who had been playing very little but won a very nice pot early on, called a raise before the flop from a very aggressive and very chatty regular. The flop came down king, six, three, and Red Shirt checked. The regular went all-in and Red Shirt immediately called. The regular was laughing as he turned over a five/ten offsuit, and he stood up and put his satin baseball jacket, emblazoned with the casino logo, on his back. Red Shirt flipped over a pair of kings for three of a kind. The next two cards were a four and a two, giving the regular a straight; everyone groaned the way men do when they see someone get kicked in the groin on television. Everyone except Red Shirt, who quickly and quietly counted his chips. He had more money going into the pot so he survived, but barely.

I had the chance to pick up a few pots here and there and had double what I started with when the first break came. After a smoke and a call home, I sought out Red Shirt to offer my compliments and sympathies. He thanked me graciously for the kindness and said, *That's poker. That's poker* is a credo of serious players who have been on the ugly end of a bad beat. It means that there will be good luck and bad, and the patient player will get his share of both.

Over the next hour, I didn't pick up a lot of great cards. I stuck it out and folded some hands that I might have played in a cash game. I moved all-in a couple of times against smaller stacks but didn't get called. Whenever I bluffed with all my chips, even if I had a small hand or a draw, I felt like players could just see right through me. I tried to stay very still whether or not I had a big hand so they could not get a read, but it was hard. When you lie, your body and mind want to do things to support that lie, like look the other player in the eye, but when you try that, something makes you look away. So I just looked at my lap and let them stare at the top of my cap.

As players got knocked out, the floorman broke down tables and moved players to empty seats elsewhere. I was moved to a table next to the bar, and I considered buying everyone a Long Island iced tea, but that would probably have cost more than the first-place prize. Before buying into the tournament, I had set what I thought was a realistic goal. Make the halfway mark and finish above 50 percent of the others. If I was successful, I would try to improve on that the next time. Monitors mounted on the walls displayed tournament information. A clock showed you how much time was left of the current half-hour round, and a chart told you what the blinds, which were raised every round, would be in the next round. The most important stat to me was the countdown, listing the number of players remaining.

Two hours and forty-eight minutes into the tournament, I made my goal. I was above the medium. I might just order those drinks after all. At the three-hour mark there was another ten-minute break. I called my wife and told her that I made my goal, and she said that she was proud of me and asked if I could win. I told her no. After I hung up, I wondered if that were true. I decided, now that I'd accomplished what I'd set out to do, that I should go for it.

All the poker books talk about switching gears, meaning changing your playing style unexpectedly to throw off the table's preconceptions about your style. If you have been playing fast and loose, tighten up. If, like me, you've been playing tight, take the brakes off and step on the gas.

Back at the table, we had some new players, so I played tight for a couple of rounds. The blinds were getting high, and soon the shorter stacks would get nervous and start taking chances. I had a moderate stack of chips but nothing that could scare the chip leaders at my table.

An aggressive regular made a big raise from the button and I called it. It was just the two of us, and he was staring me down and asking me questions. This is a very common tactic in stakes games. If the player is nonchalant in responding, he has a big hand. If he starts blabbing, he's bluffing. If he's tight-lipped, there is no way to tell. I kept my mouth shut. I didn't even look at the flop because I was too scared. The regular made a pot-sized bet—a lot of chips—and I immediately raised him all-in.

Sitting there, trying to look like a statue, is the right thing to do. If only instead of having a smoke during the bathroom break I had actually used the facilities. I had no hand, all my chips in the pot, and I was about to burst. Great.

He folded, but not without a lot of whining about what a big laydown this was for him and how I'd better have the nuts or I'd be out. I pulled my chips in, mucked my cards, and ran to the head. I now had a good pile of chips, but that was no reason to slow down my play. If I was going to win, I needed to double up, and it wasn't going to be easy or quick.

The next hand I caught aces and doubled up. It was easy and quick. I had aces on the button and just went all-in. I had been all-in the hand before, and it now looked to everyone like I had switched gears. A short stack with a pair of tens and the chip leader with a suited ace/king called. My aces stuck and I was now the chip leader, not just of my table, but of the whole tournament.

Calling raises to see flops seemed like bargains. When I caught hands, I won big, and when I didn't, I got out cheap. The blinds kept going up, and I kept winning. After a lucky run, I made myself come back down to earth and tighten up, knowing a lot of people would be playing thrive-or-dive poker and I didn't want to double up anyone. Playing tight hurt my chip stack by half, and many around me were benefiting from the loose play while I watched. But I sat tight for what seemed like hours. I watched the computer screen more than the table.

I was at the final table. I was in the money. I could win my very first tournament.

I called home and gave the good news in a fashion that might best be described as hysterical. I tried to make myself calm down but failed. I had outlasted more than 120 players to make it to the final ten.

When I stepped over the stanchion that kept out the losers and riffraff, I joined the winners and sat down. Immediately to my right was Red Shirt, and we warmly congratulated each other. His stack was four times as big as mine, but I was still glad to see him.

The tournament director laid out the prize money in cash. Tenth place would get $160, while first place would get $3,200.

I hadn't bothered to study any of the final-table strategy in the poker books, thinking I would have time to do that later. I decided to see if I could wait a round or two before going all-in. The blinds were huge and were going to get bigger. But three players had fewer chips than I did, and they might have to gamble first. For every player who went out before me, I would move up in the prize money. An off-the-cuff plan wasn't the ideal, but it was all I had. I was blessed for a while with very bad cards, making my laydowns easy. There are times, especially in tournaments, when getting bad cards is a good thing. You don't want to be tortured with a suited ace/six. Or a king/queen. Marginal hands are deadly when there is a lot at stake.

Sure enough, two players went out quickly. As much as that was good news for me, it meant that I was one of the shortest stacks at the table and everyone would be looking to bust me. When I caught an ace/jack offsuit, I moved all-in and prayed no one would call. The big stacks were disgusted to throw down their hands. They wanted to call, but they were not going to do it with nothing. I tried to look at my lap and give no indication of my hand when I heard that goddamned word, *Call*.

The caller was a woman I'll call the Dumptruck, because I'm a mean, mean person. And because THE DUMPTRUCK was written on her shirt with iron-on letters. She was a regular and her picture was on the wall. I could smell the nacho cheese on her breath from four seats away. I had been at her table earlier, and she was a loose/aggressive player who made snide comments about other people's play. I did not want to lose to her.

The good news was that I couldn't. She was the only person with fewer chips than I had, and she was the only caller. The dealer counted our stacks, made the pot, and told us to flip our cards. My ace/jack dominated her king/jack of clubs. We both caught a jack on the flop and she caught one club. And another and another.

I wasn't the only one disappointed to see me lose. The whole table wanted her sent packing because it moved everyone up the money ladder. I looked at my tiny stack and looked over at Red Shirt, who just raised his eyebrows a bit and cracked a thin smile. *I know, I know. That's poker.*

I heard my name called and turned to find my wife standing behind the velvet rope. She had raced over to see my moment of glory. Nice timing. I got up and gave her a kiss. *This is so exciting,* she said. *But where are your chips?* I pointed at the two little brown ones and the single white one. *You'll do great,* she told me.

I did, too. I went all-in two hands later and got three callers. They battled each other in a side pot, but my ten/nine of diamonds made a straight and I took the main pot. In the big blind, I caught a pair of sixes and tripped up on the turn and doubled again. I was still low but hanging in. The Dumptruck wasn't faring too well, meanwhile, and went all-in when I was on the button. I called with a pair of jacks.

If you stick around long enough, poetic justice will come calling. Her ace/queen failed to improve, while my jack of diamonds made a flush. She cried to the rest of the regulars about her bad beat and how I got lucky and sucked out on her. Never mind that she had done the exact same thing to me, the real point was that there was no time when I was an underdog in the hand. I led the whole way. I looked at Red Shirt, who gave a who-cares look. Man, that guy can talk pretty well with just his face. The blinds were raised again, and two more people went out fast. The last guy actually had a decent amount of money and tried to bluff from early position. He got called and got broke. I was again the short stack, with four players left. I tried to bluff a pot and got raised, and mucked my cards. On the big blind, which took half my chips, I found a jack/ten and went all-in. Red Shirt called with an ace/ten and sent me packing in fourth place. He gave me a sympathetic look and shook my hand.

Red Shirt went on to win the tournament, and I collected my prize, $680. At the urging/insistence of the floorman, I left sixty bucks for the dealers, who couldn't be tipped by players during the tourney because the chips have no cash value.

My wife was thrilled and I was, oddly, pretty maudlin. I was never a favorite to win, but the serendipity factor in pulling off a win right off the bat was so alluring. Fourth place is no slouch, and six hundred smackers didn't hurt. The Dumptruck felt worse than I did right now, and that made me smile. My wife and I spitballed ideas on how to celebrate and spend some of the booty. I felt better and better driving away from the casino in between a field of headstones and a Kmart.

Before now, I had thought about the World Series in conceptual terms only. The thought of actually playing in it had been the stuff of daydreams. I would allow myself to fantasize about possible scenarios that would propel me forward, like flopping four aces when someone else flopped kings full. Or getting caught in a bluff and hooking a straight flush. I never allowed myself to consider that it was possible I could actually play the game well enough to compete. Now, however, that possibility was blossoming, and I was letting it. Only a very small part of me worried that this was a mistake.

Coming in fourth in a small tournament is no monumental achievement. After all, someone came in fourth yesterday and someone will come in fourth tomorrow. But someone would win the World Series. Why not me? I'd set the bar high for my next game and my next tournament. *How can I improve from this moment?* I asked myself, and I had many thoughts on the matter. There was one answer to that question I did not consider at the time: *You cannot.*

**I can remember** my first real poker game and the first game I ever lost all my money at with the exact same clarity. Of course, they were the same game.

When I was a kid, my mother and father owned a small, seasonal resort on the Russian River seventy miles north of San Francisco. Time stopped at the Lodge, as it was commonly known, in 1966, and no one who frequented the bar and restaurant was in a hurry to restart the clock.

At the end of every school year, my parents would load me and my eight brothers and sisters into a Ford LTD station wagon and we'd go north for the summer. The older kids, of which I was one, were expected to help around the joint when needed. My older brother served as lifeguard at the pool, whereas I bused tables and washed dishes in the restaurant during busy nights. Even though the town of Guerneville was only a strong hour outside the city and survived on tourist dollars, the area residents considered themselves rural, wearing cowboy boots and chewing tobacco.

The Lodge was run by the previous owners, Dick and Midge, who oversaw all operations, and Tut, who served as both head bartender and best customer. Tut looked like Hunter S. Thompson, except he could drink more.

The busiest nights of the year were when the Sons of the Pioneers came to play. The Sons were the backup band for the singing cowboy Roy Rogers until he retired, and they kept the act together and traveled the country-western circuit. They would play a sold-out show and then play cards all night.

One night after helping to close the kitchen, I walked down to the bar, where the Sons, Dick, Midge, and Tut were setting up the poker table. I asked if I could play and was patronized, teased, laughed at, and then told no.

I had $40 in my pocket, half being my wages for dishes and half my busboy tips. I pulled it out and put it on the table. I reminded everyone that I, too, had worked all night and should be allowed to play with my own money if that was what I wanted.

One of the Sons of the Pioneers—I can't remember which because they all looked the same—suddenly agreed, and the others followed suit. Dick and Midge shrugged their shoulders. Only Tut protested, pulling me aside and pressing me to take my money and go home. He was overruled, mostly by me.

Forty dollars was enough, in those days, to merit taking. If I'd only had thirty, I think they would have let me go. Forty, however, was worth their while.

I lasted about an hour, playing every hand to the very end. The conclusion was predetermined the minute I sat down. I didn't know how to play and they did. Strangely enough, it was Tut who took the last of my chips. He might have felt bad about it, but he did it anyway. I was twelve years old.

Maybe some of the Sons wanted a little extra for their trouble, but I think they let me in the game to teach me some things they thought I needed to know. If so, it worked. I learned that the Sons of the Pioneers were a bunch of assholes. I also learned that poker is a skill game, not a luck game. Most important, I learned that losing is painful and I hate it.

*   *   *

**Winning streaks are funny.** You don't know where they come from, how long they will last, or when they will end. Losing streaks are not funny. You don't know where they come from, how long they will last, or when they will end.

Since my fourth-place finish at Lucky Chances, I found myself on a losing streak. Not one session or two, but dozens and for months. I lost everything I had won and more.

I had the poker equivalent of what golfers call the yips. Poker, with all its colorful vocabulary, has no word for it. Poker players have leaks, which are habits like drugs, alcohol, and roulette that drain their poker bankrolls and self-confidence. They can go on tilt, which only lasts for a few hands or maybe a whole night. But for a long-standing, seemingly inexplicable losing streak, the jargon is silent.

The most maddening thing was not simply that I was losing, but that I was losing and could not figure out why. If I went through a what-the-hell-it's-only-money phase and played recklessly, I could accept it and straighten up. I had many Come to Jesus meetings with myself to determine if I was too overconfident, sloppy, or presumptuous. I really did not think I had these failings, at least not at the table.

I tried to analyze how I lost to try to find a common thread. But there are as many ways to lose a hand as to win it. I lost every way, in a seemingly evenly distributed manner. I called when I should have folded, and folded when I should have raised. I played too meekly and too aggressively. I got bad cards that lost and good cards that lost. I got outdrawn. I got unlucky. I went over and over my games, what happened and when. Did I get my money in with the best cards? I remembered going all-in with a pair of kings and losing to a pair of aces. I remembered going all-in with a pair of aces and losing to a pair of kings.

Did I misread my opponents? Did I get outplayed or outdrawn? I autopsied everything looking for clues. I replayed hands in my head and on the floor with a deck of cards. I investigated hands by flipping through my reference books looking for similar scenarios to see if I played right. I replayed them on the computer. I was some sort of goddamned Quincy, except the guy who killed my game got away. Jack Klugman would never have allowed that to happen.

The worst possibility was that I was on a winning streak before and that my losing streak was actually my level of play. This was not a good thought. Self-doubt has destroyed more gamblers than cocaine and craps put together.

My losing streak began on a day like any other, except I was going to a place I had never been with a guy I barely knew. Okay, it was not a day like any other. Across San Francisco Bay was a card club I had never been to, and I thought for the sake of variety I would try playing a tournament there. They had a Saturday rebuy game that sounded fun. Rebuys allow you to purchase more chips if you go bust during the first stages, so the play is fast and loose early on. If you play tight and get lucky with some top cards, you can build a monster chip stack pretty quickly.

A friend of my brother-in-law's named Chad had sat at a couple of my home games and was a pretty sharp player. We had talked about going to a card club sometime, so one Saturday morning, I picked him up and we drove across the Bay Bridge. I had read up on rebuy strategies, which vary widely from book to book, and had decided to play sit-back. Chad said he planned on staying aggressive and buying back in if he needed to. Both strategies can work, and I was interested to see which of us did better in the same tourney.

It took a while to find the club because it was on one of those long California roads that was once a booming main drag connecting many towns before they built the freeways fifty years ago but was now a long stretch of ugly disrepair. Half the street signs were missing, and half the buildings were shuttered, whitewashed, or burned out.

The club was a well-known place for the occasional shooting in the parking lot, but since it was ten o'clock in the morning, I wasn't too worried about that. We pulled in and I decided to valet park, an extravagance that cost $2. I hoped it was an authorized valet I handed my car keys to and not just somebody who happened to be wearing a red waistcoat.

The club had an Old West theme, making its mostly Asian staff look pretty silly in bolo ties and cowboy vests. The main pit was a room the size of a prison dining hall or a Catholic high school cafeteria, and it had the same sense of social hierarchy and potential for violence. Unlike Lucky Chances, there was no familiar vibe from the regulars or staff. It felt like a big room filled with people who don't like each other. Watching a game from the rail, I noticed every flick of the dealer's wrist shot a card toward the players as if to say *I . . . Can't . . . Wait . . . To . . . Quit,* while the players didn't seem to open their mouths except to tell off the dealer or another player. Lucky Chances seemed like Romper Room compared to this place.

Chad and I shoved and pushed and got shoved and pushed to the tournament cage. I got to the gate and asked if there were still orchestra seats for *The Producers* left. To be fair, it was loud inside and he may have misheard me and thought I had called his sister a whore, which would explain his reaction. I bought my seat and got the hell out. Chad did the same.

We were at different tables, so we shook hands and parted ways. My table was a barrel of monkeys. A barrel of dead, rotting, fetid monkeys. I'd never seen so many people not having fun. It was like they were forced to be there.

I got off to a fine start by picking up a nice pot with ace/king in the cutoff seat. Ace/king is a strange hand in that it is overvalued by many players. It ranks in most novice players' books right up there with a big pair. But it is a drawing hand and needs to improve to be good in most situations. A pair of twos is a roughly equivalent hand odds-wise, and most people dump their deuces into the muck. Ace/king is nicknamed big slick, but it has other monikers too. Some younger players have taken to calling it Anna Kournikova, because it looks pretty but does not win. The old-timers call it walking back to Houston, because road gamblers who overplayed it would lose the titles to their cars and end up on foot.

I am generally suspicious of the hand and have never fallen in love with it. I'll see a flop or raise someone before the flop with it, but I want that hand over before fourth street, one way or another.

Today, though, ace/king was good to me. At least for a while. Two rounds into the tournament, I was reraised all-in with ace/king and, having too much of my stack in the middle, I called and lost to a pair of queens. I had to rebuy, but that was okay. I saw Chad doing the same thing a few tables across the room.

Not long after, I flopped a full house while an opponent flopped quads. I paid for one more go, but this was it. I played tight and was eventually moved to Chad's table. I was short-stacked, but he was doing just fine, until he fell in love with an ace/jack suited and his flush draw never came through. I was out only a moment or two later.

*Fuck this place,* I told him as we grabbed a beer at the bar. *I know where we can find a soft game.*

*Oh, yeah. Where?*

My sister's house was recently rebuilt, remodeled, and renovated by my father. What had started life as a modest farm-house in a sleepy town was now a palatial home in a tony suburb with one of those kitchen islands big enough to accommodate a performance of *Cats*.

My sister and her husband were hosting a barbeque for some occasion and had invited me, my wife, and our son. I had already had plans to play poker, so my wife and son went over to feast and play. Much of my large family would be in attendance, more than enough to sit a game. I had promised to come over after the tourney, if I didn't wind up at the casino too late. Being at the casino late is good news because it means you are in or approaching the money.

I called my sister's house and asked if anyone would be interested in some poker. A quorum would not be a problem, but they had no chips or cards. Chad and I stopped at an enormous drugstore and bought some cheap plastic chips and some expensive plastic cards and drove across another bridge.

We ate, had a couple of beers, and rounded up the players. My kid brother, two sisters, my mother, my cousin, and my wife joined the table. After my wife, who knew poker as well as anyone can who doesn't think it is important, the only other one who knew the rules was my little brother, who had learned the game from TV. Chad looked ready to go, and I made a bank and collected twenty bucks from everyone.

I had played in enough games with newbies to know not to try to bluff. Chad, however, had to learn that one the hard way, and he lost half his stack before tightening up a bit. You don't bully people who have just learned to play because they want to play all the way to the last card.

The good thing about new players is that while they will call anything, they rarely raise, so I called a good number of minimum bets trying to catch a nice flop. Chad tightened up so much he would not call from the small blind, fearing that the big blind would raise. It was a wise strategy for the card room but a little risk-averse here.

My mother kept asking if anything was wild, but I knew that was a ruse. She is a very competitive player in any game and, after she knew the rules, she knew the game. My stack dwindled while I waited to make a hand, and I finally caught an open-ended straight draw. I bet and got three callers. The turn brought my straight and I checked. One of my sisters bet and everyone called, including me. I wanted to raise, but I wanted the others to catch up. On the river, I bet and got two calls and a raise. I raised again and everyone called except my mother, who went all-in. I called and the others folded after no small amount of deliberation. I laid down my straight, and my mom asked if her flush beat a straight. She knew.

I bought back in. The strategy was sound, but I really needed to pay more attention to the board. I could have survived that if I had just called the first round of betting. Lesson learned, I thought.

The next person to take all my money was my wife, who had three of a kind to my two pair. My sister took Chad's last buck with a full house. Of the seven players at the table, five left as winners. I didn't talk much on the way home, except to ask my wife for bridge toll money. She was up $40, the big winner, and could afford it.

Perhaps it was some sort of cosmic payback for trying to bust my relatives, but the streak continued. I laughed it off at first, just some bad luck and into each life a little rain must fall and so forth. I even made notes on what I had done wrong so I would not repeat my mistakes. I went back out to the church game and lost the tournament as well as several seatings at the losers' tables.

I found a game with a bunch of very nice, very drunk Irishmen and, as always with drinking games, avoided bluffs and stuck to good cards. I got cleaned out. I hosted another home game and ended up having to write some friends checks to pay my unders.

Online, I wasn't doing much better. Instead of making the money once every three times, I was getting a payday every ten times, which put me negative. I tried jumping up to higher-stakes games and down to easy-money games. I lost regularly at both.

I reread my books, played my simulations, and reviewed my notes. Nothing seemed to work. I was lost when I played the cell-phone game.

I knew enough that if I pressed myself to a point that I no longer enjoyed playing, I was doomed. I might as well go back to that nasty casino across the bay and become a scumbag.

I took a break and laid off for a few weeks. I just needed a breather, I told myself, and the ill winds would die down. Ending the losing streak had risen to a new level of importance. I had signed a deal to publish my book. This was not a surprise. My agent had loved the idea when I pitched it to her many months before, and I have one of the few agents in the business who never says she loves something unless she does. I wrote up a proposal explaining how I envisioned the book, and my publisher's reaction was enthusiastic. Then came the negotiations, followed by an agreement, and finally a contract. The signing of the contract was mere formality, but it got to me.

I was through the roof in most respects. I had a great editor, the support of one of the world's biggest publishing houses, and an advance that would pay for my entry into the World Series of Poker, not to mention quite a bit of keno on the side.

I was nervous as hell too. My crazy idea was now translated into a legal document. I had an editor, a publicist, and a deadline. The series was coming up in two short months, and my recent poker exploits were becoming a cautionary tale.

Trying not to think about poker made me think a lot about poker. Even if I wasn't playing or reading, my mind would wander back to a particularly bitter hand. Every time I turned on the television, there was another tournament full of players, professionals and amateurs, who were actually winning. But over time, I thought about my losses less and less. Whenever I was reminded, I'd try to remember the words of Red Shirt and try to find the humor in the situation.

Going back to Lucky Chances a few weeks later, I was a little nervous but convinced that my losing streak had to be long behind me. I had come to the conclusion that the only thing wrong with my game was that when I walked into a game, I walked in expecting to lose and that was manifesting itself in undetectable ways that caused me to lose. It was thin, but that was my story, and I was sticking to it.

I brought with me a good friend whom I had mentored somewhat in poker. I didn't tell him that I was on a losing streak because it would have made him nervous. He had played at a couple of casinos but never ventured into no-limit. We signed up and he got seated first. I had to wait thirty agonizing minutes until a seat opened. As I went to my table, I saw my friend sitting there with a big pile of chips. The seat had opened because he had cleaned somebody out. I bought in with my only hundred, as I wasn't going to throw good money after bad if I lost, and sat down. It was a good action table, but the talent wasn't intimidating. I played others' hands in my head and saw some tasty flaws I could exploit if I got the cards. My friend was either playing more aggressively than he had planned on or he was getting some great cards. I folded hand after hand. Sometimes I dumped immediately, and sometimes I waited a few contemplative moments so the other eyes would find me and see me fold. I wanted to establish my image as a rock so that when I made a play, it would be feared.

When a player in fourth position raised $10, an amount double the big blind, which was a relatively small and suspicious bet, and was flat called by both a very loose player and my friend, I decided to make a play for the pot even before seeing my cards. This may seem reckless, but if you sense weakness and don't act on it, you will never succeed in No-Limit Hold 'em. You have to play your opponents as much as if not more than your actual cards. I had a good read on the first caller, and he made small raises with a weak ace. The loose player had folded several times to a raise if a hand was live behind him. And this was my friend's first real game, and I had told him I was going to wait for premium hands.

When it got to me, I looked at my hand, put a chip on top indicating a bet, and raised the size of the pot. I felt confident in the play and in the way I executed it. Losing streak, my ass. The button, both blinds, and two raisers all folded.

My friend moved all-in over the top.

I looked at him. I hadn't expected him to soft-play me, but I didn't think he would go for my throat either. I looked at my cards again, buying time: eight/two offsuit. It wasn't the worst hand in poker, it was the second worst. He stared at me like we had never met. I was only Hollywooding before dumping my hand and giving him half my chips, but in the moment I waited, I saw him as a player and not as a friend. He looked at me sternly for a moment then suddenly looked away. When he raised, he had slammed his chips in the center of the pot. He held his cards like he was more than ready to flip them as soon as he was called. He had to be bluffing.

I called time and leaned back. If I really put him on a weak hand, why did he call the raise and not reraise it? Did he have a hand that he liked a lot with one other player but not four and want to see if the flop helped him? A small pair would do that. But he, or anyone else, would simply call my big raise, not go all-in. He could have medium suited connectors, like seven/eight or nine/ten, because you can make a lot of money off those in multiway pots if you make your hand. We had talked about playing those in the car on the way over. Suited connectors were a definite possibility. Or he could be on a stone-cold bluff and have called the bet so he could make a move on it later after the loose player bet at it. That's a moneymaker if you have the stones to pull it off. Could he make a move like that at his first game of casino no-limit? Knowing him, sure.

I had all that information and no way to call. Unless he was going all-in with the worst hand possible, I was beat. I would have loved to call with my last dollar and try to suck out on him. But that was the wrong decision. I folded and tapped my palm on the table to say nice hand. I had only $25 left and had no intention of going back for more. I would lose today like so many other days before, but, oddly, I didn't feel bad. I was right to attack those weak bets. I was right to fold when I was raised. I did not win the pot, but I made the right decisions. All the poker books sang the same chorus on this one. Poker is not about winning and losing; the game is about making the right decisions. The winning will fall into place by itself.

I stuck at the table waiting for a hand but saw very little that interested me. The blinds ate at my stack for two rounds, and I got up and left a minute before the rake was collected since there was little sense in paying $6 for another half hour when I would only have nine bucks left. I tipped my dealer well and went to the bar.

My friend joined me half an hour later with an apologetic look on his face and three racks of chips. I smiled and shook his hand. He started explaining that he had planned on making a move on those same two players and was very sorry I got in the way. I assured him I was fine with it and he could buy me a beer. It was impossible not to enjoy hearing a new player gush about how much fun No-Limit Hold 'em is. He asked a lot about tournaments and we made plans to play in one together.

He said he was sorry again about the hand.

*That's poker.* I shrugged. *By the way, what did you have?* He looked chagrined and told me he had a seven/eight of diamonds. He figured I was bluffing.

*What did you have?* he asked.

*Kings,* I said. *Don't do that again or you're going to get broke.* He nodded.

That's poker, indeed.

 **Texas Hold 'em first** became cool with the 1998 release of the movie *Rounders*, starring Matt Damon and Edward Norton. The movie captured beautifully the intrigue and nuance of the game, but, more important, it made a persuasive, honorable case for being true to your own nature—namely, quitting law school and leaving your prissy girlfriend so you can play cards with gangsters. A morality play for the ages, in my eyes.

Chris Moneymaker was the first amateur player from the new generation to win the Main Event of the World Series of Poker. He won his seat in a $40 online satellite and credited *Rounders* as the reason he began playing. He made millions and quit his job as an accountant. Between Moneymaker's feat and the movie, hundreds of thousands of people were inspired to take up the game, providing a solid audience base for the televised events and the burgeoning Internet gambling sites.

If the movie made poker cool, television made it hot. An essential part of life is watching television. This is particularly true for poker players now that tournaments are aired practically twenty-four hours a day. You can watch pros playing other pros, pros playing amateurs, celebrities playing each other, celebrities playing pros, and, if you are desperate, race-car drivers playing professional bass fishermen and the biggest names in Arena Football.

The most popular poker show on television is *World Poker Tour*. The show proudly proclaims that it broadcasts real tournaments from exotic destinations all over the world, which is especially true if you consider New Jersey, Mississippi, and California exotic. To be fair, there are a few locales that can legitimately be called international, including a Mexican cruise, two Caribbean ports of call, and the Aviation Club in Paris. But no one really cares. I, for one, am less concerned about where a game is played than how it is played. I would rather watch chimpanzees play poker in Peoria, Illinois, than watch *American Idol* or *Will & Grace*.

*World Poker Tour*'s main host is Mike Sexton, a guy who was lucky enough to sign on the poker ship at the end of its golden era. With his neat hairdo and double-breasted suits that don't shimmer or shine, Sexton looks more like an FBI agent or a high school principal than a gambler. He is known as a solid player, someone who lacks gamble but doesn't make a lot of costly mistakes. His participation gives the show a lot of credibility, unlike his cohost.

The cheesy beau hunk that sits in the broadcast booth next to Sexton is Vince Van Patten, the son of Dick Van Patten whose claims to fame are playing the Bionic Boy and gracing a few spreads in *Tiger Beat*. The only acting he does now is acting like he's famous. And he's bad at it.

The third and fourth wheels on the show for three seasons were Shana Hiatt's, *ahem,* personal attributes. Ms. Hiatt played the part of the requisite poker babe, interviewing players as they lost and helping lesser babes bring the prize money to the table when it came down to heads-up play. The show replaced her in 2005 with a blonde version and kept the same wardrobe of tight, low-cut party dresses.

The proliferation of televised tournaments can be traced back to the United Kingdom in the late 1990s, when a BBC producer came up with the idea of using the new technology of lipstick-sized cameras embedded in the cushioned rails of the poker table. Suddenly, television viewers could see the hole cards and know if a player was bluffing or holding the nuts. *World Poker Tour* was the first show to bring lipstick cameras to American television.

The real gift the hole cameras gave to the game was making the game look easy to novices and recreational players. Viewers with the benefit of knowing everyone's cards, and even the win/loss percentages on each hand, said to themselves, *This game ain't so tough. I could beat these guys.*

Notable among the suckers that held this belief was me. With the gift of omnipotence that the cameras provided—meaning I was able to see everyone's cards—I convinced myself that poker success could be mine. I watched tournaments and marveled at the large prize money. *I could do that,* I thought. I wasn't alone.

What I, and millions like me, forgot is that television is a lie. We saw the final tables, where even last place paid a fortune, but we conveniently forgot that for every winner there were hundreds of losers. We saw the money moving back and forth across the table every hand but did not notice that, thanks to deft editing, there were eight hands in a row where everyone folded to a small bet or the big blind. Ignoring all warnings, people like me started flocking to the tables and organizing home games.

Previously, Texas Hold 'em was exciting to play because it had the most action—many hands per hour, the most money, et cetera— but boring to watch, because so many hands were folded before there was a showdown, where the players had to display their cards. The 1997 World Series of Poker was televised with every bell and whistle ESPN could think of to make it exciting. They put the final table in the middle of Fremont Street under the giant neon awning that runs the length of the block. Many poker players consider this event to be the best in poker ever, with Stu Ungar's unlikely comeback and the mix of styles at the table. But unless you were already a poker fanatic, it was a bore. At one point, the camera panned over to a player's wife, and she was asleep in the bleachers while her husband was in a hand for more than $1 million. When the special lipstick cameras were added, viewers could watch the drama play out regardless of whether the cards were ever laid faceup. Before the cameras, ESPN or the Discovery Channel televised a one-hour synopsis of the World Series. In 2005 ESPN televised twenty hours of World Series of Poker events, including Omaha, Razz, Seven-Card Stud, and Limit Hold 'em. The Main Event was given twelve hours of coverage and replayed with alarming frequency.

Today, people are so hungry for poker games they're willing to watch B-list "celebrities" who don't even know how to face each other at the table. My guilty pleasure is *Celebrity Poker Showdown*, a basic cable show featuring wannabes, has-beens, and where-are-they-nows playing terrible poker while comedian host Dave Foley makes gay jokes and poker commentator Phil Gordon cringes at the bad play. The show usually begins with Foley introducing his famous guests.

*And now, playing for the Ventura Center for Elective Surgery, is Angie Dickinson, who is, as you can see, still alive. Please welcome, from the WB's* Teenage Angst in Suburban Bumfuckegypt, *Madison Mackenzie Meningitis, playing for the Tony Franciosa Skin Care and Facial Tic Clinic. Pauly Shore, ladies and gentlemen, is here playing for his rent money.*

*Next week, please tune in when we're joined by the remaining cast of* Mama's Family.

As a rule, I have little tolerance for celebrities. I can appreciate an actor's work, but, given our present climate of beatifying the famous, I have very little sympathy when they act like crybabies. Getting free clothes, cars, and vacations just for being famous isn't enough. Having every door opened for you and both your ass cheeks kissed by everyone you come in contact with doesn't do it. Twenty million dollars for ten weeks' work? Sure, it's nice, they say, but not nice enough to mitigate having your picture taken constantly in public. Celebrities want to live in the limelight but have control over the switch. If you want to be king of the jungle, fine. But even lions have to deal with hyenas if they want to eat the whole zebra by themselves.

The line between poker and celebrity is getting fuzzier all the time. Poker players are expected to sign autographs at airports and shopping malls. Danish player Gus Hansen was voted one of *People* magazine's sexiest people alive in 2004. Phil Laak is poker's clown prince, a guy so over the top that even pros who despise showoffs can't help but make an exception for him. He is known as the Unabomber because he wears a hooded sweat jacket and shades, making him look like the FBI's sketch of Ted Kaczynski. Kaczynski might be pissed off at the dehumanization of industrialization in society, but I bet he's more irked at having his menacing nickname co-opted by a jocular spaz who dates a movie star. Laak is shacked up with Jennifer Tilly, the Oscar-nominated actress, giving him Hollywood-style notoriety. Tilly, under Laak's tutorage, has become a fantastic poker player, winning the World Series bracelet in the Ladies Event and the WPT Ladies Night trophy.

Ben Affleck is a decent player who won one major tournament, the California Poker Championship in 2004. But he was a serious chump for years before that, losing perhaps millions at the tables to the best pros at the Bellagio. Being a chesty celebrity, he was able to befriend some of the game's best players, such as Annie Duke, and solicit criticism and advice. Meanwhile, his bankroll is fat. If he goes broke, he just dons another red jumpsuit and dangles around in front of a blue screen for a few weeks and—presto—he has another $20 million check. He's a good player now because he spent more on his education than Harvard Medical School's class of 2006.

Tobey Maguire is another pretty boy who dabbles in serious poker, but the best compliment he can be afforded is that he plays okay for an actor. He never gives interviews when he is anywhere near a table, and he's been known to run in to a tournament, take his seat, get busted, and leave without ever saying a word to anyone.

For the old-school actor-gamblers, like Telly Savalas and Gabe Kaplan, it took years for them to garner serious Vegas respect. It was probably easier for Kojak because he was a high roller who looked tough in a tuxedo, whereas Mr. Kotter, never a pretty boy, now has blistery, pocked skin and a patchy Afro beard that makes him look scary.

Given that the ability to disguise your own damn self is such a plus in poker, one might think that actors would make great poker players, having at least an added edge starting out. Clearly, many actors agree, as the game is riddled with them. Famous names and faces are lice on the scalp of poker. Except, as a rule, they're not sucking blood but providing fresh stock for poker pros around the world. Why? Because they are good at acting, not at not acting. Every celebrity I've seen interviewed about card playing is asked if their thespian training has helped them at the table, and they all say yes in some manner.

I would say no.

Acting is a dangerous proposition at the table. The chances of being able to hold up a false tell for minutes on end while a pro stares you down looking for any crack in the facade are not good.

You smile when you're happy, you cry when you're sad. You laugh when you're amused, and you get angry when you see Vince Van Patten (but maybe that's just me). The natural thing to do when you take an action is to convey that emotion in total, every element of communicative sense backing up the other. In poker, you want to take what is natural and train yourself into believing it is unnatural, simply because it is unprofitable.

When you have the goods, you want to be nonthreatening, if not invisible. You don't really care what someone else has when you can't be beat, so you don't pay much attention to the other guys. You want them to call or raise you. When you bluff, you're trying to project strength.

A player has only two choices. He can act or go dead. Acting is staying engaged in the game, talking and moving and trying to be an enigma by overwhelming the opponent with conflicting information. An actor will talk throughout his, and others', hands in the hopes that another player will be so confused he will fold, call, or raise back. Going dead is just shutting down, staring at a fixed point, unblinking, denying any possible information. An opponent will send test flares up trying to get a reaction, like *Whadda ya got, kings?* The favorite probe query is, *Do you want me to call?* The audacity and absurdity of the question can often draw a glance, if not a comment. A good reader of tells doesn't pay much attention to what his opponent says, but how they say something or act can speak volumes. I know this from experience, but not because I have strong reading skills. Rather, when I'm playing against someone with keen reading skills, I seem to be playing with my cards faceup. The only way to combat a reader is to shut down.

This is what many actors cannot do well. They can't sit still and disappear into the background withholding emotion. It's counterintuitive to someone who seeks the spotlight to consciously disappear. They cannot read tells very well, with a few exceptions, because they are not used to paying attention to anyone but themselves.

Hollywood actors never consciously project an asshole table image. I would guess that they feel their own celebrityness is image enough or they're afraid of bad press. If they do act like assholes, I believe it's because they are assholes. This is all conjecture on my part, but I was soon going to have a chance to test it out. Live from Las Vegas.

**With book contract in hand,** I went to the organizers of the 2005 World Series of Poker asking for a press pass. They sent me an application asking if I was a member of the print, radio, television, foreign, or Internet media. I wrote *other*. It asked if I was working on a news article, a feature, a documentary, a poker blog, or other. I wrote *other*. Under the space for media affiliation, I wrote Penguin

Books. There was no option for writing a book and no space to describe my project. I was worried that I would be summarily denied.

But I was approved and received a note saying my press pass would be waiting for me at the media check-in desk. As a surprise bonus, I had been deemed important enough to rate an entry ticket to the Celebrity/Media Tournament, a one-day affair where the famous mixed it up with the great unwashed who were assigned to cover the WSOP. Each participant would play on behalf of a charitable organization. The winner's charity would receive $10,000, and the winner would get a plaque.

When I arrived in town, I took my ticket into the press room, where someone held a clipboard protectively to her chest. I presented my ticket and she gave me a table assignment and asked what charity I was playing for, and I realized that I had no answer. I thought about using the People Fund, the fictitious organization made up by George Costanza on *Seinfeld,* but there were too many television types around that would catch on. I chose Planned Parenthood, to get in good with my pro-choice wife and piss off Pat Robertson.

*Can I ask if there are any celebrities at my table?* I said. Expecting some magician or tap dancer under contract to Harrah's who needed a little exposure, I was pleasantly surprised when she scanned down the list and said, *James Woods. Do you know who he is?*

Truth be told, I felt lucky to have James Woods at my table. Of all the celebrity pokeristas, he is one of the best. He has a solid, selective/aggressive game. I had seen him as a guest at the Heads-Up Championships, and I thought he held his own with some of the world's best. Besides, there were plenty of no-talent hacks who were being passed off as celebrities. The tournament director tried to introduce all the *famous* entrants with equal enthusiasm, but he couldn't even pronounce some of the unfamiliar names.

Walking to my table, I tried to see all the glorious celebrities around the room. There was Penn Gillette, the rotund magician and well-known skeptic. I admire his show *Bullshit!*, on which he attacks pseudoscientific crap like feng shui and astrology. Oddly, he has a long ponytail and was wearing some sort of African muumuu, making him look like a New Age kook. Dick Van Patten looked old and cranky, probably because he is old and cranky. Brad Garrett, the hulkish comedian from *Everybody Loves Raymond*, and teen masturbatory fantasy Shannon Elizabeth were there, as was someone named Nicole Richie, who I think is Luther Vandross's daughter.

I found table nine and took my seat. I was jazzed for this tournament. If there's one thing a writer should be able to count on it's that writers are smarter than actors. Actors are notorious for being bad at managing their money and for having their money stolen from them, usually from their business managers or their parents, depending on the actor's age. Writers, meanwhile, are the smartest people in the room generally, and if they lose all their money it's usually because, in time-honored traditions, they drank it or spent it on hookers, horses, or ex-wives.

All of us at table nine were beginning to think Woods was a no-show, but he made it to the table just as the dealer was going to skip his hand. He apologized and took his seat. For a while everyone was quiet and focused on their cards, but after a few hands things started lightening up.

Woods made a point of engaging every other player, either by complimenting their play or commiserating on a bad beat. This wouldn't have been obvious if he had not decided to do it in order from left to right around the table. He insisted everyone call him Jimmy. When, every ten minutes, a camera crew came over to interview him, he would grimace slightly and glance around the table, as if to say, *Sorry, guys. I want to play poker with you but I can't be rude.* I sympathize with the idea that being yourself is tough when everyone wants a piece of you. Celebrities need to develop a set of protocols that allow them to react in a manner found palatable by fans but that still doesn't take too much out of them. This manner may not be phoniness, but it's not real, either.

Earlier, I had thought about what I might say to Mr. Woods, now Jimmy, that wouldn't seem unctuous or stupid. I mused about telling him how great I thought the movies *True Believer* and *Salvador* were, but I was afraid that might remind him that he hadn't done anything great in the past few years. I wondered if I could engage him on politics, where we disagree on many issues because he doesn't think George Bush is a retard. He might consider such provocative conversation interesting and brave. Politics at the table is dangerous ground, and surely everyone would have an opinion, surely leading to blah, blah, blah. I then tried to figure out a way to slip the line *Sean Young is a twat* into the conversation, but an opening for that was unlikely.

We had been playing uneventful poker for a couple of hours when I decided I should make a move. I was in the small blind, the worst spot to play from, and if I had pocket aces I would still think twice about playing a hand. A crazy young guy was in the big blind, and the first to act was Jimmy. He looked at his cards for a moment and put his elbows on the rail, as he had done every time before. He had a serious look on his face, like his agent had just come to him with an absurd but very lucrative offer to play the wacky pathologist on *CSI: Muncie*. He looked at his chips and then glanced at everyone else's stack. He took half his chips and shoved them in the middle. Jimmy had taken so much time to make his bet that several of the other players had used the pause to glance at their cards, so when Mr. Famous bet, they dumped their cards without thought.

Normally, when a player raises in the position known as under the gun, it denotes real strength. To bluff from the crappiest spot is the act of a solid fool or a reckless genius. At a ten-person table, there are nine other guys to act after you. If you call, you've raised the profit margin for everyone else. If you make a small raise, at least one person will see the opportunity to represent aces—or actually have aces—and raise you up big. It just sucks. The only legitimate hand to have under the gun is aces, because if anyone raises or calls, you're still the favorite. And many times, there's some sap with a pair of tens who feels like raising 'cause he hasn't seen a real hand in hours or he's short-stacked and needs to take a risk.

It was odd that I was in this position again. On the round previous, the guy sitting to Jimmy's left had gone all-in under the gun. And I had called him with an ace/ten suited from the cutoff seat because I felt he was making a move. But Jimmy didn't see this. He had stood up and stepped aside to give an interview to some poker television show. When he sat back down, now in the same position as the guy I busted out for making such a weak-ass move, he didn't know that playing a loud bluff from first position wouldn't play. He made a big raise, like he was inviting someone to call or go over the top. Everyone folded to me, and I raised him all-in. I must have looked at my cards because you have to, but I don't even remember what I had. This was a move that had proven to be poison earlier, and if Jimmy missed that fact, he was in trouble.

James—sorry—Jimmy looked at me and studied me for a long time. It was the longest he had looked at anyone or anything during the tournament, except, of course, Shannon Elizabeth, who was under constant study by most of the men and some of the women. I knew he was going to fold. If he'd had a real hand, he wouldn't have made such a blunder as raising big from a bad position; he would have slow-played them to entice some action rather than scare it away.

The act of pretending to sweat out a big decision is called *Hollywooding* in poker. The coincidence didn't escape me. I kept my best poker face, not knowing what look I might adopt to make him fold his hand. He counted his chips to see if he was pot-committed, meaning that he had so much of his stack in play that he might as well call. I knew now he wasn't totally bluffing. He must have some sort of hand, a small pair perhaps. It was a borderline decision because he'd still have a few good bets left if he folded, but nothing that would scare someone away if he bet. I also guessed that Jimmy did not want to go out early. Neither did the rest of us, but he certainly would not want to be the first celebrity out, because he was known as a good player. So he could not play the aggressive poker he is known for.

He looked back at me with genuine annoyance. I suddenly felt sorry for him, which is always a mistake in poker. My face must have betrayed me because he grabbed his cards and flicked them toward the dealer. *Nice bet,* he said.

I wondered why he folded now and realized that he saw a slight twinge of pity in my eyes. *Should* I be sorry for having a better hand than the celebrity? Why would I want one of the beautiful people to leave the table? If I had better cards and was obligated to raise, then I *should* be sorry. I was annoyed.

After that, Jimmy entered a few pots cheaply, trying to catch a nice flop, but it didn't work. He was severely short-stacked and would soon be going all-in with, most likely, a less than premium hand. I no longer cared about engaging him in conversation. I just wanted to bust him.

I didn't get the chance. Jimmy was knocked out in short order by a reporter for one of the new poker magazines. He shook everyone's hand, posed for some pictures, and headed off. I think now that it was impossible for Jimmy to be a celebrity and a poker player at the same time. You can't expect to meet the media obligations, glad-handing all the schmucks, while playing serious poker.

Now that my table was celebrityless it was a little sad. The cameras were no longer around, the chatter died out, and faces hung. No one would be discovered at table nine this day. Even the dealer had a hangdog face.

I buckled down to play some serious poker and went broke on the next hand when I got caught bluffing.

**The Rio Hotel** and Casino is, for Vegas, nothing special at all. At roughly thirty stories high and sitting a quarter mile off the strip, the building looks a bit like a hip flask sticking out of the sand. The exterior is pin-striped (read: classy) by red neon (read: sexy). The name Rio shimmers day and night, trying to entice customers with the exotic allure of Rio de Janeiro's Carnival minus the transvestites and street urchins. Anywhere else, the building would be a spectacle, but in this town, it was nondescript.

I was in Las Vegas to pick up my World Series of Poker Main Event championship bracelet, although I still had to go through the formalities, like besting thousands of others in town for the same reason. I had one hundred hundred-dollar bills that I hoped to turn into seventy-five thousand hundred-dollar bills.

Fresh from Las Vegas McCarran International Airport with my wife and son at my side, I stood in line at the cashier patting my inside pocket, where my ten Gs were stowed, to make sure I hadn't lost the money just yet. I was a little scared that someone might be able to tell I was carrying such a bundle of cash until I realized that every one of the people in line had at least the same amount of money in their pockets. When I got to the cage, I handed the woman $10,000 and she handed me two white pieces of paper and called, *Next*. One piece of paper was a ticket to the world championship at table 172, seat 3, of day 1B, and the other was a coupon for $10 off the cost of a buffet lunch. They looked exactly the same.

My wife and I walked into the main room, which was still being set up. It was like an airport hangar with chandeliers, hidden cameras, and table seating for twenty-five hundred. It took me fifteen minutes to find which would be *my* table because it was right in front of me, where I never look. What was nice was that in this sea of tables, I was on the edge near the gallery, so my wife would be able to stand by her man as I achieved poker glory. And she could be there to stop me if I tried to end my life after busting out.

I was very happy that by the luck of the draw I had been assigned to the second first day. Even with this massive room, they couldn't accommodate all the entrants, estimated at more than five thousand players, at once. They had to split day one into three fields, designated days 1A, 1B, and 1C.

Day 1A was my son's fifth birthday, and I wasn't going to be playing poker while he was opening his presents. I had his birth certificate in my back pocket, and if I was randomly selected for 1A, I was going to find someone important and badger them until they relented and let me switch. Either that, or we were celebrating at table 172 and the other players could help blow out the candles.

With nothing else to do there for many hours, we left the Rio and headed back to our hotel to check in. I had brought my entire poker library, thinking I would be able to read everything one last time so I could finalize a winning strategy. Now that I was here I had a lot of hope and I believed I was due for something extraordinary. I could win it.

I wondered how many people were thinking the exact same

thing right then. At the time, it was a hypothetical question, but later I learned the answer: 5,618 other people had the same notion.

**One might think** that a person training for a year to compete in an incredibly expensive and important event would be certain to be on time for it. One would be wrong. The WSOP ticket said 11:00 a.m. on it, but the woman who checked me in told me noon was the starting time. The extra hour was just a buffer period, like at the airport. It sounded reasonable. I mean, who shows up two hours early as requested to go from Phoenix to Denver?

I had planned on getting there early anyway. I was still stinging from my foolish loss the night before at the celebrity tournament, and I wanted to find out who won. I had not stayed to watch others succeed where I had failed. Now I also wanted to get the lay of the land, visit the press room and introduce myself to the tournament staff, interview some professional players, and look in on the WSOP trade show going on next door to see if I could wrangle some free stuff.

As we walked toward the convention center, my wife and I were passed by people running at full steam. I didn't think that much of it at first, until some of those people running seemed to be putting their lives in danger. I saw someone with a staff badge and grabbed him to ask what time the tournament actually started. *Just a minute ago,* he said. He started to say something else, but we were already racing away.

The World Series of Poker was not enough splash and splendor for Harrah's, which owned the Rio. In the same convention area they were also hosting a *Star Search*–type talent show for children. Before we could make it to the poker room, we had to dodge and weave scores of sequined, high-strung children in makeup and high heels and their parents, who stood there criticizing them.

I jumped over the velvet rope that served as a barrier between the players and the gallery. Without slowing down, I slid into my seat like Bo Duke gliding into the General Lee, except that I missed and knocked my chair into the table, startling everyone.

My eyes toured the table, sizing up my opponents as they did the same to me. I was in seat three, and to my left was a twenty-five-year-old with very bad skin and a Poker Stars hat on. Next to him was a husky fellow with a buzz cut and a sports jacket. Beside him was a guy I silently nicknamed Sporty, who also wore online garb. Down the line a bit was a gray-haired gent in a powder blue golf jacket. Then came the Greek, a man with a rusty tan and as much jewelry as a straight man is allowed to wear, and the Geek, a guy who tried to hide his Ultimate Bet T-shirt with a zippered sweatshirt. Seat ten was occupied by Frenchy, another big guy from, say, France. On the other side of the dealer was a man who had jet-black hair, a very neatly trimmed mustache, and a really pricey watch. Lastly and directly to my right was a fortyish Asian man who looked vaguely familiar. Maybe he was from the Bay Area and played at Lucky Chances. Nope, that wasn't it. I knew him from television. And magazines. He was a poker pro. His name was David Chiu, and he was one of the best.

I wanted to see all the pros I had gotten to know on television. I was not alone. People were stopping everyone who looked vaguely familiar to ask for an autograph. I saw a man who looked like, but was not actually, the powerhouse player Amir Vahedi signing a program and then laughing to himself after the mistaken fan had gone. While I would have loved to talk to a pro, I certainly didn't want one at my table, especially one like David Chiu. Mr. Chiu was a renowned cash-game player and only played tournaments on occasion. He had made a couple of televised final tables over the last couple of years. But he hadn't been exposed enough to be recognized by the masses. I was convinced I was the only one at the table who knew who he was. That would have suited him just fine, I was sure. Then his cover was blown when T. J. Cloutier, one of the most recognizable faces in poker, stopped by our table to say hi to him.

To the pros, people like me are called dead money. *Dead money* is a term for people who contribute to the prize pool without any real chance of winning. When poker was first becoming a popular phenomenon, the pros loved dead-money players at their table, or any table for that matter. A few weaker players would be carved up by the others and sent packing. Eventually, there was so much dead money that it became tough for the pros to get through them all and end up at the final table. The dead-money players changed too. Many players who entered the televised tournaments played superaggressive poker, knowing they needed to double up constantly or face elimination. Even if they didn't play aggressively in general, some just played directly at the pros, thinking, *I might not win, but I'm going to have a story to tell by beating or going broke to a poker icon.* Pros started having to defend their stacks constantly and found themselves all-in too many times, even against weaker hands or long-shot draws; it only took one bad beat to ruin their chances.

In very big tournaments like the Main Event, all the pros say that the important thing is just to survive the first day, not to build up your chips. Dead money, by sheer numbers, has turned the tables on the pros and made them afraid. Often the reaction by the pros is to complain that dead money exacerbates the luck factor and lessens the skill levels.

Phil Hellmuth, known as Poker Brat for his spoiled, whiny behavior, is one of the best players in the world. If it wasn't for luck, he says, he'd win every tournament. This is, of course, a dig at amateur players, but it is also an insult to his fellow pros.

I thought of a way to put Hellmuth's theory to the test. It's a game I invented called Hellmuth Hold 'em, where if you call an all-in bet, the cards are flipped and whoever has a higher percentage probability of winning at that point in time wins. No more cards will fall. If the all-in occurs on the turn, then the cards are turned over and a calculator comes out. My bet is that Phil would win about the same percentage of times that he does now because he misreads, gets trapped, and sucks out on par with most of the top pros.

In a way, my table was perfect, a representative sample of the World Series. There were three online qualifiers, two foreigners, two rich guys, one old-timer, one professional, and one fraud. We all had a chance—maybe not an equitable one, but a chance nonetheless. Everyone there saw themselves a week from now on top of the poker heap, and the march to glory would begin with the hand the dealer was now passing out. Nine/four offsuit. Well, my march to glory would begin with an easy laydown.

Three minutes later, I saw a man a few tables away get up. He had his coat in his hand and a small duffel bag full of, I suppose, snacks and supplies for a long day. He shook some hands and walked out of the room. All eyes were on him, but he stared straight ahead. He was over sixty, balding, and looked a little like my father. He was the first cautionary tale of what eventually would be thousands. I don't know how he made it to the doors without falling apart. Losers are a very common sight in Vegas, and the veterans are steeled to their plights, but there wasn't one player in that room who didn't feel for the guy.

I would love to regale all with my brilliant plays of the first hour, but I didn't have any. The only hand I won was the time the blinds were folded to me. The second hour would prove more exciting when I did actually play a hand, making a small raise on the button with a pair of tens and taking the blinds. I didn't mean to play that tight. I was playing to win, but I never got a hand until the tens. I watched everyone's play and wrote down their hands when they had to, or chose to, show them. There were no odd plays here. People played tight poker, and if they bluffed, they never got caught. It was, so far, the most boring game I had ever played in.

During the break, I left to have a smoke and use the can. The World Series has been a nonsmoking event for many years. I guess the muckety-mucks who were making the case that poker is a sport worthy of television coverage and mainstream sponsors folded to the powers that be who said it can't be a sport if you can smoke while doing it. Golf and bowling are victims of this too. So no more smoking at the tables. But this is Vegas, where they have ashtrays in the elevators. Even if you cannot smoke on the tournament floor, you can smoke everywhere else. During bathroom breaks, people would stream out of the front doors, cigarettes in hand and lighters at the ready. The minute they entered the hallway, they fired up. It was a little funny to me that the people who hated smoke were screwed. If you had been able to smoke in the huge ventilated room, the offensive fumes would have risen harmlessly away. The hall was much smaller and not nearly as airy, so everyone had to endure the fog of Marlboro vapors. If the building had caught on fire, no one would be able to tell. When I made it through the smoking hordes, I didn't even need to light up, so I looked for the bathroom.

The tournament's being held in a convention center had many advantages, but restrooms weren't one of them. They had plenty for a normal event, such as a trade show of five or even ten thousand people. But the WSOP was a little different. Everyone had to go make water at the same time or lose money by taking a break during play.

After the break, I returned with a new strategy. If I wasn't getting playable hands and had to keep laying down, I would use my table image as a tight player to my advantage. I would wait until there were a couple of calls or a single raise in front of me and go after the pot. That would refill my chip stack, which had been reduced by the blinds.

A couple of hands later, I was in the small blind and decided to pull the trigger. I didn't even want to look at my cards for fear they would reduce my confidence level. A move based solely on my table image had to look natural and scary. I decided to raise the bet to $900, about 10 percent of my chip stack, and $200 more than most raises had been. The Geek, Frenchy, and Mr. Chiu had called the $100 big blind, and when I announced my raise, it was the first time most of them had heard my voice all night.

*Call, call, call.* It happened so quickly. Bad Skin called from the big blind, and the Geek and Frenchy seemed to say the same word at the exact same moment. I had been sitting in my seat for the past two hours like I had just downed a bottle of cough syrup, but now I was sitting up dumbfounded. And it was not over yet. Mr. Chiu was still to act. Whereas the others might have been caught up in the fast-moving moment, Mr. Chiu was going to move at his own pace. He looked at all the players for a moment and at me for two. *Raise,* he said quietly. *Fold, fold, fold, fold.*

They say you are lucky if you can survive one mistake in the World Series as long as it is not a big one. I had just made mine.

Over the next hour I stayed tight. I watched as money moved back and forth. I was only a spectator when Bad Skin went all-in with a pair of sevens and got called by Sports Jacket's pocket aces. Before the flop, we all listened to Bad Skin stand and cheer optimistically for a good flop. When that didn't work, he demanded a seven to show itself on the turn. Blank. He begged the river for help. Bad Skin was out, but he didn't leave. The dealer pushed up the cards that made for Sports Jacket's winning hand, but Bad Skin just strained to see if a flush or straight was there somehow. Sports Jacket shook his hand, and we all murmured something to the effect of *Good game.* The dealer yelled, *Open seat—172.* The cards were gathered and shuffled, but Bad Skin was still there holding the back of his chair. We went back to playing and acted like he was gone, which he was.

My patience, or fecklessness, was rewarded when I landed a pair of queens in the small blind. I would have liked a better position, but two ladies is the third-best starting hand and I was not going to dump them. I had called a few bets and seen a flop or two, but I had not really played a hand and I was ready. Frenchy had called the big blind, but he was the only player in so far. I had about $7,500 of my original $10,000, so I bet $700. Sports Jacket, one of the biggest stacks at the table, raised it to $2,100. Frenchy folded. Sports Jacket had played very few pots, but the only time he'd had to show his cards, it was the pair of aces. Suddenly, my third-best hand didn't seem so strong. I thought about going all-in but talked myself out of it damn quick. His raise seemed borderline between wanting me to fold or call. I decided to press. I raised it another $2,100 and he called. I put him on an ace/king.

The flop—the crappy, loathsome, backstabbing flop—came down ace/king/six. I hate this fucking game.

He could easily have put me on ace/king too, so I checked, hoping he would do the same. He bet $4,000, which was more than I had. I took a very long time to make a decision, and he didn't seem to mind. All the pressure was on me with that flop, and I decided that this just wasn't my hand. I folded. If I had a table image at that moment, it was that of a wussy. I could be bullied; in fact, I was practically begging for it. This was a live table. I would never, and will never, know if I was really beat.

I had only $3,200 in chips left when a meal break was called. I was the first one away from the table, and I felt like never going back.

Food was abundantly available if you were willing to walk six miles uphill to the food court. If you wanted a bite near the games, there was a mini-mart across from the main hall that reminded me of a 7-Eleven, except for the prices. My Snickers and a Coke were, I think, $400. I considered using my $10 buffet coupon instead of keeping it as a souvenir, but another player told me the meal cost $30 and the restaurant was in another zip code. A makeshift food line had been set up near the main entrance selling hamburgers in foil bags that someone had made back in 1977, but the end of the line was a fifteen-minute walk. So back to the mini-mart, where a delivery man had just wheeled in a load of sandwiches encased in those triangular plastic containers that one might find for sale at a gas station. The crowd lunged at them before the shopkeeper could check the order and sign the invoice. The delivery guy grabbed the sandwiches out of people's hands and threw them back in the bin. After the embargo was lifted, we dove in.

I ended up with a ham and cheese that had not yet passed the expiration date. Jackpot! I took a second mortgage on my house to pay the bill and joined my bride in the hallway to feast on my bounty. We found a quiet spot—just kidding—and squeezed in between two throngs of sweaty people and had a little picnic. I wolfed the grub like an animal. This morning, I had $10,000 in my pocket, and now I was eating garbage food on the floor, and I didn't care.

I had been playing for four hours and was already exhausted. My wife, who had been on her feet standing right behind me, was fresh as a daisy. Since my mouth was full of stale bread and something that purported to be meat, she did all the talking. One by one, she gave me her impressions of my tablemates and what she thought their styles of play were. She went over several hands to illustrate her point. Her recall was perfect and her reads made a lot of sense. Four hours into the tournament is not the right time to realize that the wrong player is in the game.

She told me my queens were good. She had been able to see my hole cards from behind my back and was convinced that the hand was mine if I had called. What about the Greek, I asked. *He was full of shit*, she said. *He had nothing.* She may well have been right. I half hoped the botulism from my sandwich would act quickly and send me to the hospital. A stomach pump sounded great right now.

I don't know how long exactly we talked, but I suddenly realized it had gotten very quiet. The hallway was no longer loud or crowded. We raced back into the main room to find the tournament had restarted some time ago. I jumped the stanchion and plunked down in my seat. *Glad you could join us*, Gray Hair said. He had to be a high school teacher. Mustache asked if I had a side game going on somewhere else.

*Sorry. I just wanted to play a quick nine holes*, I said. The online players both believed me.

I had to make a move. The blinds had been raised again, and people were playing their hands quicker as they became more comfortable. I landed an ace/queen of spades. The great Doyle Brunson says that he loses more money on ace/queen than any other hand. But I couldn't sit and be blinded out. I had to win a hand somewhere, somehow. I raised a third of my stack.

The man who replaced Bad Skin could have been his twin. He was a very strange guy, constantly asking people what cards they had folded and why they played a certain way from the cutoff seat, and so on. Nobody gave him any information, or if they did, they lied. He didn't seem to mind, he was just glad to be there. It was like he got in free. When he joined our table, he had about six thousand in chips, and now he had only a few hundred less, having played a lot of hands and won one nice pot.

Bad Skin II called my bet and the others folded. The flop— the glorious, wonderful, orgasmic flop—came down with a queen/ queen/ten. I wasn't stupid enough to settle for the meager pot as it stood. I checked and he checked. The turn was a jack, which meant that pocket jacks, pocket tens, or an ace/king had me beat. All four suits were represented, so no flush was possible. Although I had a few outs to make a full house, I wished I had bet my three ladies before the turn, but that was history. I announced I was all-in.

The dealer stood at the ready. When there was an all-in call, he was supposed to shout it out loud so the ESPN camera crews could rush over if they liked. Bad Skin II started talking a lot about what he thought the board read. This told me he didn't have the straight. He began babbling so fast I couldn't even hear what he was saying. I only caught the last word. *Call.*

The dealer screamed out. I stood up. I looked behind me at my wife, who was smiling.

*You got the queen?* Bad Skin II asked me, and I knew I was ahead in the hand. *Yep,* I said.

I turned over my ace/queen and he flipped an ace/ten. I'm no good at math most days, but I was like the Rain Man right then. He needed a king and only a king. There were four kings in play out of forty-four cards. That was an eleven-to-one shot against. Another ten would give us both full houses, but mine would be bigger. I watched the dealer count down the pot. He straightened the board and tapped his fist on the table twice before burning a card. I lost it. I called out for a low card. No paint. No paint.

I saw that the river was a face card before I could tell what it was. I knew in my heart that I had just lost to a king before it hit the table. I pressed my eyes shut. Everyone made surprised and shocked noises. Even the ever-silent Mr. Chiu said, *Wow*. I opened my eyes and resolved to hold it together at least until I could get out of there. *Nice hand*, Bad Skin II said. I looked at the table.

The face card was a queen.

I had never had four of a kind in a live game before. Playing the computer game, I once had four aces beat by a royal flush, and that was so exciting I had woken up my wife. I was on fire now. I kissed my wife and jumped back into my seat. I had about $6,500 in chips. Not a monster stack by any means, but it was like my weight in gold to me. My comeback had begun. I could win this thing. I would win.

The next hand, I was on the button and still high when I was dealt a king/ten of hearts. There were no raises when it got to me, so I called. If I couldn't win with a big pair, perhaps a trapping hand would work. The flop came down king/five/eight, with the eight being the only heart. It was checked around to the Greek, who raised $1,000. The others folded to me and I called. I could have raised but could not, with my chip stack, make myself do it. It was just the two of us when the five of hearts fell. I now had a flush draw and top pair, and I wanted to win the pot right there. I looked at my dwindling chips and grabbed $3,000 and put it in front of me. The Greek didn't hesitate for even a moment. He moved all-in.

My good feeling from a minute ago was gone. Sick as I was, I bore down and tried to determine what he could have. I had top pair and a flush draw. But he was betting not just like he was unafraid of the king but like he was unafraid of the flush. He could have a king with a higher kicker, made trips, or two pair. Unlike Sports Jacket, the Greek was impatient. I could not use this as a read because he was impatient with everyone during every hand he was in. He wasn't staring me down like a bluffer or avoiding my gaze like he had the nuts. He was acting exactly like he was betting—he had a big hand. I went with my gut. He had it. He had at least three of a kind and probably a full house. If I wanted to prove it, the price was all my chips. I folded.

I went into the third break and tried not to think about that last hand. I walked around with my wife trying to talk about anything but poker. She played along like a sport, and we talked about what an amazing spectacle the whole affair was. I marveled at the organization of it all, considering that a convention of the American Association of Anal-Retentive Nitpickers would be an easier crowd to please.

How could they keep it organized and moving forward without a disaster taking down the whole thing? The tournament directors, some of them mere kids, had to monitor the play at two thousand tables at once, with every player on edge and having a great deal to lose. Meanwhile, hundreds of untested, short-timing employees were on the edge of revolt. I saw players and spectators bending the ears of officials about not being able to smoke, while others complained about the smoke drifting in from the hallway.

To make it interesting, dozens of camera crews were roaming through the aisles looking for any conflict. Many of the dealers, I guessed, were hired as temporary help. During my time at the Main Event, I heard more job complaints than when I served as a union shop steward. One bitter woman, who railed at the tournament directors for leaving her at the tables for three hours at a stretch, decided to slow down the play. One player got up, whispered in someone's ear, and was quietly relieved for a break, or maybe she was taken out back and roughed up. Either way, we were happy. Forget about the dealers, the floormen looked like they hadn't had a break in three years. Oh, and they had to make sure that no one said any naughty words.

This was the first year the higher-ups, perhaps mindful of poker's new respectability as family entertainment, banned the use of what they called the F-bomb. The F-bomb is the word *fuck*—perhaps you've heard it? It is a great word, and there are times when, for an exclamatory, no other word will do. What do they expect at a poker table? Someone who gets drawn with runner/runner says *fuck* and another player at the table will wail, *Oh, my virgin ears,* and faint? This is not a Christian day camp; it is high-stakes poker and it is rated R. If the word *fuck* bothers you, go play bingo at church.

The penalty for dropping the F-bomb was expulsion from the table for ten minutes. When the blinds are huge or you are coming in to good position, this is a stiff punishment. When Mike "the Mouth" Matusow was questioned about possibly flicking his cards toward the dealer too forcibly, a floorman was called over. The other players attested that Mike had thrown the cards at the muck, not the dealer. But while waiting for a decision, Mike mumbled, *I don't fucking believe this.* The floorman tossed him. Mike's response, *I don't fucking believe this,* got him another ten minutes' rest, to which he pointed out, *This is fucking bullshit,* which made it a full half hour. Mike wasn't done. *I can't believe this fucking shit.* He still ended up making the final table.

This rule is really a shame. Poker is a fine venue for the word, and its expulsion from the table without consideration of context is wrong. But what the fuck do I know.

I made it back to the table early, before the break was over, and counted my chips ($1,700) and the blinds were going up again. I had gotten away with a couple of mistakes, used up my Mulligan, and got my miracle hand. If I had a chance now, luck would have to be the deciding factor. I sat and waited quietly and wished I believed there was a god, and that he answered poker prayers.

A few minutes later, I found myself with a pair of wired fives. Frenchy had raised the pot to $700. I went all-in and he called. The dealer once again shouted, but there were no camera crews around. The all-in calls that once caught our attention were now occurring every few seconds, and no one paid them any heed.

I showed my fives, and Frenchy turned a queen/ten of clubs. I was actually a very slight favorite. When the flop came four/four/nine with only one club, I began to feel excited again. The turn was an ace of clubs. Mr. Chiu said, *Even money,* quietly. The eight of clubs was my river—and my good-bye. I shook hands with Frenchy, who gave me a what-are-you-going-to-do shrug.

*That's poker,* I said.

Mr. Chiu told me that I played a good game. I thanked him and left.

It was over.

**The hallway was always** the center of activity. During the breaks, people milled around just cruising the scene. Pros mingled with the online qualifiers, and girls in half shirts shilled new gaming Web sites. The sea of potential champions made for a sober but excited Mardi Gras. But as the actual tournament progressed, the mood changed. The happy hallway became the passage of sorrows.

When you lose all your chips, you are no longer welcome. This is understood. It only takes a minute to move from player to spectator. Then you have to leave. For these guys, it took all their remaining strength and dignity to wish everyone luck and walk off without breaking into tears. Many had to be chased by the staff with the coats, bags, and iPods they'd left behind. By the time they got off the floor and stepped into the hallway, emotions had often gotten the better of them.

Walking the hallway with my consoling wife, I watched the dozens of men and women lining the passage, leaning against the walls and telling their bad-beat stories on their cell phones. They could no longer contain themselves, and many of them were crying. They could not bring themselves to leave, though, hoping against hope that a tournament director would race out after them, saying there had been a terrible mistake.

I looked sympathetically at one who was lying flat on a bench. He was splayed out with one arm dangling to the floor while he covered his face with his other hand. He saw me watching him, and I gave him a sympathetic nod. He flipped me the bird. That's the spirit, big guy.

My wife was proud of me, not just for lasting this long, but for doing it at all. My son was proud of me too, mostly for taking him to someplace that had a pool, but still. . .

I would think a great deal about my last hand over the next few months. If only I had called his $700 and then raised the additional grand, he would have folded. I ran this past a few friends who cared about such things. Some of them said he would have folded; others said he would have called anyway, figuring he was getting the right pot odds with two overcards to the board. Most said maybe, maybe he would have laid it down.

I can take some small pride in getting all my money in with the best hand. I can say I did that at the World Series of Poker against the best players alive. I did that, but it doesn't comfort me much just to have a legit bad-beat story.

My fantasy was not fully realized, but it did come true, even if it was only for five hours and five minutes. If nothing else, I grabbed the fucker and dragged it from fiction to fact. It isn't a dream anymore if you make it happen, and I did that, and that will remain true long after they load the final table into a backroom.

I might have grabbed my coat and walked out without looking back. But I didn't need to pretend to have somewhere to go because I did. I was going to frolic in the pool with my wife and son and enjoy the sunshine. Then, after everyone was asleep, I would figure out how to come back next year. I would find a way to crack this game.

Or not.

# Epilogue

**It has been a few months** since I came within a hairbreadth of winning the World Series of Poker. A hairbreadth in this case meaning several thousand players and seven full days of play, but it's my book.

For a few weeks, I found some semblance of pride in the fact that I outlasted many famous pros, including Johnny Chan, Daniel Negreanu, Chris "Jesus" Ferguson, and a dozen others. As much comfort as I can find in the misfortune of others, it is still hard to think about it. I replayed the hands, two specifically, that kept me from poker glory and my fantasies of owning a whole bunch of stuff I don't need.

None of the one hundred players picked as favorites by the very respected *Card Player* magazine made the final table except for Mike "the Mouth" Matusow, and he was the first one eliminated. Most of the players had some strong experience with professional poker but nothing close to the established pros.

For me, the last two days of the tournament were, oddly, a distracting thrill. The final table was a fourteen-hour marathon, the longest in WSOP history, but it seemed to me far too short. The winner was the polite and gracious Joseph Hachem, an Australian mortgage broker who was encouraged to pursue his dream of winning the tournament by his wife, who stayed at home with the kids while he played. That sounds familiar.

It was the second-place finisher, though, who inspired me more than Mr. Hachem. Steve Dannenmann was a thirty-eight-year-old accountant from Severn, Maryland, who bought his way into the tournament with the help of a buddy, with whom he agreed to divide any unlikely profit. Mr. Dannenmann described himself as the fourth-best player at his weekly home game. He wore the same lucky shirt every day of the tournament and called his wife after every big hand. He was a bit of a goofball. Everyone knew it, but he did not apologize for being thrilled by every moment. He loved being there. Every step closer to the championship increased his joy, and it showed. He was having such a great time that he went out of his way to remind the other players that they might want to consider doing the same.

On the felt, Mr. Dannenmann played a solid/aggressive game. When entering pots, the man did so with good cards and bet them if they improved. He had no tricks or slick moves that I could tell, and he didn't depend on luck to get ahead. He was a very solid player who loved the game and the spectacle.

This is why he did so well and why I failed. Mr. Dannenmann was excited. I was nervous. He played the game like it was a pleasure, and I played the game out of fear. He told himself that the only way he could lose would be if he didn't have fun. I never considered fun. Coming in second place was in no way a disappointment to Mr. Dannenmann, and neither would have been coming in five-thousandth place.

**After taking a few months** off from poker, I'm starting to play again—and I'm winning. I am going back next year, and I am going to do a lot better than I did this year—regardless of what place I finish. I hope I get seated with Mr. Dannenmann because it would be a lot of fun to bust him out.

# Recognitions and Thanks

**My wife, Jeannine,** and my son, Jack, deserve as many thanks as one man can muster for helping me with this book.

Amy Rennert is the best agent in the country and is quickly becoming the best poker player. Louise Kollenbaum too.

Thanks to the crew at MacAdam/Cage, especially David Poindexter, for doing me such a big favor. Jason Wood's help was valuable and much appreciated.

Caroline White of Penguin is the stone-cold nuts.

I would also like to thank the makers of Red Bull energy drink, Slim Jim unrefrigerated meat snack, and Parliament Lights cigarettes, without whose fine products the writing of this book would not have been possible.

Finally, to the staff and organizers of the World Series of Poker, I offer my gratitude and respect for a wonderful experience. See you next year.

# Poker Glossary

**aces**

The most powerful starting hand in Hold 'em is a pair, or so I'm told, as I rarely get dealt them, and when I do, I lose. It is rumored that the first player out in World Series play every year is someone who had their aces beat by a lesser hand.

**aces up**

Two aces and another pair.

**action**

  a. A player's turn to act. When the dealer tells me that the action is on me, it means it is my turn to make the wrong decision.

  b. Frequent bets and calls. A player who gives action is one who is willing to gamble more than prudence dictates.

**active player, active hand**

A player still involved in a pot.

**all-in**

To bet everything you have. *All in* are the two most powerful and terrifying words in poker, other than *Don't shoot*. If the amount of one player's chip stack is less than another's bet, then a side pot is established.

**ante**

A usually small contribution to the pot made by all players. Hold 'em uses the blind structure until the late stages, when an ante is added to force more betting by increasing the pot size.

**baby**

    a. A low card. A baby ace is the top card with a low kicker.

    b. A term of endearment or derision or both. Usually preceded by *Who loves you* or *Don't be such a. Baby* is to Las Vegas what *dude* is to California.

**backdoor**

A hand made by both the turn and the river card to make a drawing hand. *See also* runner/runner.

**bad beat**

To get all your money in with the best hand, only to see another player get lucky.

**bad-beat story**

The most common and tiresome thing in poker. The always annoying tale of how every single player, if you ask them, got knocked out of a tournament.

**bankroll**

A poker player's stake, used exclusively for playing.

**belly buster**

An inside straight draw with a silly name. Also called a gut shot, in keeping with the gastrointestinal distress theme.

**bet**

Money put forth by a player in a poker game. Duh.

**big blind**

The forced bet made by the player two spots left of the dealer.

**big slick**
A nickname for ace/king.

**blank**
A card that is turned that doesn't seem to affect anyone's hand.

**blind**
    a. A forced bet by certain players before any cards are dealt. The idea is that before the cards are dealt, everyone pretends that the first person to act, the guy to the left of the dealer, makes a bet. The guy to his left doubles that bet. The action (see above) then falls to the next player, who can fold, call, or raise. The blinds take the place of an ante and stop someone from sitting all night and waiting for a pair of aces before playing.
    b. How drunk I get after losing a lot of money.

**blinded out**
To sit tight and not play any hands as the blinds rotate around the table, diminishing your chip stack.

**bluff**
To bet like you have a big hand when you have crap. I never do this. I swear to God on my eyes.

**board**
The community cards that are exposed by the dealer.

**bottom pair**
The lowest pair between the board and your hand. If you hold ace/three and the flop is king/queen/three, you hold bottom pair.

**broadway**
An ace-high straight.

**brush**
An employee of a casino or card room who assists the players in getting seated and changing tables, and otherwise accommodates them.

**bullet**
An ace. The letter *A* looks like a bullet, get it?

**burn, burn card**
The dealer, before displaying the flop, turn, and river, discards the top card. This is done to prevent players from somehow catching a glimpse of the uppermost card, although it is hard to imagine that they could.

**busted**
To lose all your money.

**busted straight, busted flush**
A drawing hand that does not mature.

**button**
The puck designating which player would be the dealer if the deck were passed around.

**buy-in**
The cost of entering a tournament.

**call**
To match a bet or raise.

**calling station**
A player who shows very little aggression by calling bets but rarely raising.

**case card**
The one and only card that can help my opponent's hand, which appears with mathematically alarming frequency on the river when I play.

**change gears**
To alter your style of play to throw off other players' perception of you.

**check**
To pass when it is your turn to bet.

**check-raise**
To pass and then raise after another player makes a bet. Also called sandbagging.

**chips**
Thin slices of potatoes, deep fried, and often dusted with delicious flavoring powders, like barbeque and cool ranch. Mmmmm. Also, french fries in the U.K. only.

**chopped pot**
A tie. The pot is divided equally between two of more players.

**connectors**
A hand where the two hole cards are only one apart, such as an eight/nine.

**cowboy**
A king.

**cracked**
    a. When a top pair, usually aces, is beaten by a lesser hand.
    b. The poor man's *Mad* magazine.

**cripple**
When a player loses most, but not all, of his chips.

**cutoff seat**
The player to the right of the dealer; the second-best spot.

**dead money**
Players who contribute to the prize pool of a tournament without the skills to be considered contenders. *See also* Walsh, Pat.

**dealer's choice**
Home-game protocol where the rotating dealer gets to choose the game. This option invariably leads to games like Indian Poker, where players hold cards against their foreheads.

**draw, drawing hand**
A hand that is incomplete pending the exposure of additional cards.

**drawing dead**
A hand that cannot win even if it improves dramatically.

**fifth street**
The last card exposed in Hold 'em. Also called the river.

**fish**
A bad player.

**flat call**
To call, usually when you have a good hand but want to disguise it. Also known as a smooth call.

**floorman**
The guy in charge at a card club or casino who tells you to put your shirt, shoes, and socks back on even though this is a free country goddamnit.

**flop**
The first three community cards, put out faceup at the same time.

**flopping a set**
Holding a pair in the hole and having a third match appear on the flop. They tell me this is a nice thing to have happen.

**flush**
Five cards of one suit.

**fold**
To lay down your cards and quit the hand.

**fourth street**
The fourth card exposed by the dealer. Also known as the turn.

**full house**
Three of a kind and a pair.

**glossary**
A list of terms and definitions in the back of a book that can be instrumental in a writer's ability to make his tome thicker without doing a great deal of extra work.

**heads-up**
One-on-one poker.

**hole cards**
The cards dealt to you and only you.

**kicker**
An unpaired card used to determine the better of two hands that are otherwise equal in value. If two players have the same two pair, the one with the highest spare card of five wins.

**limp, limp in**
To merely call.

**loose player**
A player who enters pots with less than premium hands and raises and bluffs frequently.

**maniac**
A very loose player.

**muck**
The discard pile. Also, the act of throwing away your hand.

**nuts**
The best possible hand at a given moment. If the board is six/ seven/eight and you have a nine/ten, then you have the nuts. If, however, the turn is another eight, then the nuts have changed because someone may have a full house or even four of a kind. *See* stone-cold nuts.

**offsuit**
A starting hand with two cards of different suits.

**on tilt**
The state of being where your decision-making process is damaged by a past hand, usually a bad beat.

**open-ended straight**
A four-card sequence where a card could complete the straight on either end.

**out**
A card that will make your hand win. If you have an open-ended straight draw, like seven/eight/nine/ten, a six or a jack will complete your hand, and you have eight outs (four sixes and four jacks).

**overcard**
A card higher than any card on the board. If you have ace/king and the flop is ten/five/two, you have two overcards.

**overpair**
A pair higher than anything on the board.

**paint**
Face cards.

**play the board**
To use only the cards showing on the board as your hand.

**pocket**
Your hole. Wait, that sounds nasty. The cards dealt to you.

**pocket pair**
Two like cards in your hole.

**post**
To put in the blinds.

**pot**
The money in the center of the table.

**pot-committed**
Having so much of your money at stake that you have to call a bet.

**pot-limit**
Games where the maximum bet is the amount of the pot. Pot-limit is the middle ground between limit and no-limit.

**pot odds**
The relationship between the amount of money needed to call a bet relative to the chance of winning the pot. If there is $40 in the pot and someone bets $10, then the pot is paying you five-to-one odds if you call. But if you figure that your hand is a ten-to-one underdog to win, then the pot odds are unfavorable and you should fold.

**premium hands**
High pairs and high suited connectors in the hole.

**quads**
Four of a kind.

**rags**
Bad cards.

**rainbow**
A flop that contains three different suits, killing the likely possibility of a flush.

**raise**
Up the bet.

**rake**
The money paid by a player to a card club or casino to pay for the privilege of losing, although sometimes the rake is a percentage of a pot siphoned off before being awarded to the winner.

**read**
To deduce which cards another player holds.

**rebuy**
The option to buy more chips in a tournament.

**represent**
To pretend to hold a specific, usually premium, hand by betting big.

**rhabdocoele**
A turbellarian worm with an unbranched intestine, having nothing to do with poker or gaming at all.

**riffling**
The act of shuffling your chips from two stacks into one using only one hand. Riffling is considered, at best, showing off by those of us players who cannot do it very well.

**ring game**
A cash game, as opposed to a tournament.

**river**
The last card to join the party on the board. Also known as fifth street.

**runner/runner**
The turn and river cards, which combine to complete a hand, usually your opponent's.

**rush**
A lucky run of cards.

**sandbag**
To check-raise.

**satellite**
A tournament wherein the prize is a paid ticket to another tournament.

**set**
Three of a kind with one on the board and a pair in the hole.

**sheriff**
A player who frequently calls to prevent others from successfully bluffing.

**short stack**
A small amount of chips relative to the amounts of the other players.

**showdown**
The moment of truth, when cards are turned over to see who won.

**side pot**
A pot made when one player is all-in but other players still have the option of betting between them.

**slow-play**
The opposite of bluffing. To act like you have a lesser hand than you do.

**small blind**
The smaller of two blind bets and the first player to act in a hand after the flop.

### soft-play
To play weakly against someone because they are your friend. A polite form of cheating.

### solid player
A very good, and very dangerous, player.

### splash the pot
To throw your chips into the pot, making it difficult to determine the amount of the bet or integrity of a call.

### split pot
The division of a pot when two or more players tie.

### stone-cold nuts
The best possible hand, bar none. If you hold a jack/ten of clubs and the flop is eight/nine/queen of clubs, there is no possible hand that can beat you no matter how many cards are left to come.

### straight
Five cards in numerical sequence.

### straight flush
Five suited cards in sequence.

### string bet
A bet or raise done in two motions that allows the bettor to gauge a reaction from an opponent before committing to a particular amount. String bets are illegal in all professionally run games.

### table stakes
The rule that no one can play with any money not brought to the table originally or earned during play.

### tell
A physical trait or action that betrays what a player holds.

**toke**
A tip for a dealer in a cash game.

**top pair**
The highest pair between a hole card and the board.

**trips**
Three of a kind.

**turn**
The fourth community card. Also known as fourth street.

**under the gun**
The player in position to act first.

**wheel**
A straight from ace through five.

**whinge**
To whine and complain shamelessly. *See also* the entirety of this book.